**JB JOSSEY-BASS™**
A Wiley Brand

# Fundraising Strategies for the Small Shop

Scott C. Stevenson, Editor

**WILEY**

# Fundraising Strategies for Small Shops

Published by

## Stevenson, Inc.

P.O. Box 4528 • Sioux City, Iowa • 51104
Phone 712.239.3010 • Fax 712.239.2166
www.stevensoninc.com

## TABLE OF CONTENTS

# Fundraising Strategies for Small Shops

## GETTING STARTED: BASIC FUNDRAISING STRATEGIES

*Beginnings can be difficult. Whether you are entering the field of fundraising for the first time, starting in a new organization or position, or just launching a new program, getting started presents a unique set of challenges. The following articles present a range of hints, tips, strategies and procedures to get any initiative off on the right foot.*

## Getting Started When There's No History of Giving

If your organization has little or no history of generating gift revenue, the time couldn't be better to establish a development program. But if your charity is like many just getting into fundraising, the entire responsibility probably rests with one individual.

Here's your recipe for getting a fundraising program up and running:

- **Put it all in writing.** Develop a yearlong written plan. Draft an operational plan that lists fundraising goals for the year and breaks those goals down into quantifiable objectives. Include a master calendar that identifies every step that will occur throughout the year to reach your objectives.

- **Assemble a core committee of determined volunteers.** Ask a handful of individuals who believe in your cause and have experience to help you with fund development. Their job is to help identify, research, cultivate and solicit gifts. Be up-front about the focus of their work.

- **Assemble a mailing list along with a series of direct mail appeals.** Include those who are already connected to your charity in some way. Review annual contributions lists of other charities; who among them should be included on your list? Once your list is assembled, plan for no fewer than two mailings during your fiscal year asking for gifts for a specific project.

- **Market an annual gifts (or membership) program.** Collect annual gifts literature from other nonprofits. Evaluate what it says and how they delineate giving levels and accompanying donor benefits. Then create an annual fund (or membership) brochure of your own.

- **Secure a three-year challenge.** Who, among those you know, has the ability and interest in making a challenge gift — preferably over a three-year period — that would match any new or increased gifts to your charity? A challenge gift will result in your first major gift and help to leverage other new and increased gifts from others.

- **Schedule regular face-to-face calls.** Make weekly face-to-face calls a high priority. Call on businesses/individuals on your own, and get your volunteers started making calls as well.

- **Coordinate a distinctive special event.** With the assistance of an additional group of volunteers, initiate an annual special event as a way of attracting new supporters, generating additional gift revenue and getting your charity's story out to the public.

Evaluate your progress toward goals monthly and make adjustments as needed. Use your first year's success as a springboard to increase your development budget, considering adding personnel and increasing next year's totals.

## Starting a Development Program From Scratch

Is your charity overly reliant on government support?

When officials with The MIND Institute (Albuquerque, NM) found their government funding was going to end, they realized they had a lot of work to do. The organization had never done any fundraising, had no donor database, and its staff, including Executive Director Kathy Burrows, had no fundraising experience.

"We didn't even know enough about ourselves and fundraising to be able to tell consultants what we wanted them to do," says Burrows. And since their funding came from the government, they couldn't use existing funds to hire a consultant for fundraising purposes. "We had to get an outside source for seed money to start the process," she says.

So Burrows began educating herself about fund development. She spent a day at the Association of Fundraising Professionals (AFP) talking to consultants who did fund development start-up. She met with organizations similar to hers with a track record of success to learn what they were doing right. She attended fundraising seminars.

For help writing a request for proposals for hiring a consultant, Burrows turned to the Minnesota Medical Foundation. Officials there helped her write a proposal that would attract consultants interested in helping within her organization's $50,000 budget, and she was able to hire a consultant. "The foundation helped us create a realistic goal for what the consultant could do for what we could spend," she says.

MIND officials started to put their fundraising program together and determined what to do first, Burrows says. Their first step was to educate board members about the fundraising process. "I talked to board members during meetings about fundraising and what it entails," she says.

"We've found that it has been easier to get board members involved in development if we can tell them what they need to do and why," says Burrows.

*Source: Kathy Burrows, Executive Director, The MIND Institute, Albuquerque, NM. Phone (505) 272-7578. E-mail: kburrows@unm.edu*

## Building Donor Relationships That Last

Development officers are fond of declaring that fundraising is all about relationships, but all too often that platitude is built on mistaken assumptions, says Simone Joyaux, author and principle of Joyaux Associates (Foster, RI): "Numerous gift officers and board members think they are supposed to solicit wealthy friends or acquaintances — regardless of whether they care about the organization's cause — simply because they share a personal or professional relationship. This can strain friendships and is not a sustainable approach to fundraising. The relationship has to be with the organization itself to last."

The key to building lasting relationships is putting the donor at the center of everything you do, says Joyaux. To do this, she suggests four steps:

1. **Develop a donor-centered corporate culture.** Being donor-centered does not conflict with being mission-centered; successful organizations can and should be both.

2. **Get to know your donors.** Learning your supporters' interests (and disinterests) is central to maintaining a donor-focused attitude, says Joyaux. Seek to understand the motivations and aspirations of the most loyal donors — regardless of gift size.

3. **Produce donor-centered communications.** Fundraisers need to put away the academic writing they used in college and embrace the principles of journalism, says Joyaux. "Read books and articles on marketing communication and focus on your audience. Don't write about your organization and its programs, write about your donors and what they accomplish through your organization and its programs."

4. **Create extraordinary experiences.** Engage and involve your major donors. Have a board member call and thank donors for their gifts — without an additional request. Ask why they chose to support your organization and use the story.

*Source: Simone Joyaux, Principle, Joyaux Associates, Foster, RI. Phone (401) 397-2534. E-mail: spjoyaux@aol.com. Website: www.simonejoyaux.com*

### Avoid Donor-indifferent Behaviors, Mindset

The abysmal state of multi-year donor retention rates — currently around 50 percent — stems in large part from donor-indifferent behaviors, says Simone Joyaux, principle of Joyaux Associates (Foster, RI). Among the behaviors she says to look out for are:

- Communications that focus on the organization instead of the donor.
- Delays in sending thank-you letters for donations or no thank-you letter.
- Carelessness in spelling donors' names.
- Failure to correct account errors, even after a donor communicates corrections.
- Ignoring donor requests to be solicited only once a year.
- Ignoring donor permission to solicit multiple times a year.
- Failure to personally engage donors at fundraisers and other in-person events.
- Contacting donors primarily or only for solicitation.

To improve donor loyalty and retention, Joyaux says, go beyond surface-level actions to focus attention on attitudes that caused or allowed problems in the first place.

## When Developing Donor Relationships, Don't Overlook Other Nonprofits

When considering potential donors, many fundraisers get stuck in the mind-set that only major business entities will be in a position to give to their cause.

Such an approach may be shortsighted.

Keep in mind that giving is a major part of the mission of many clubs, faith-based organizations and other not-for-profit groups of all sizes. So it makes sense to consider them as viable donors to your cause.

So how does one go about soliciting a nonprofit organization? In many ways, the process is no different than soliciting a business or individual: The key is to develop meaningful relationships that result in a mutual benefit, says Carol Kline, executive director of development and the Jefferson College Foundation (Hillsboro, MO).

"It's about finding the kinds of places that have a similar goal," says Kline, whose school recently entered into a scholarship agreement with her local chapter of the Philanthropic Education Organization (PEO-FR). In the agreement,

PEO-FR sponsors an annual scholarship at the Jefferson College, and in exchange, the Jefferson College Foundation maintains the scholarship on the administrative end. "This makes it easier on them," says Kline, "and we know that we can count on them for that gift every year. Everyone benefits, and it is a commitment we will share forever."

Kline calls this sort of mutually beneficial work friend-raising; the only difference between nonprofit donor cultivation and business cultivation, she says, is that both parties in a nonprofit-to-nonprofit relationship already speak the language of the fundraiser. So rather than years of wining and dining, there are years of working closely together on projects in which both parties are already invested. Eventually, the philanthropic relationship blossoms naturally.

*Source: Carol Kline, Executive Director of Development and the Jefferson College Foundation, Jefferson College, Hillsboro, MO. Phone (636) 797-3000. E-mail: ckline1@jeffco.edu.*

## Five Rules for More Successful Fundraising

The difference between adequate fundraising and outstanding fundraising is often smaller than you think, says Jean Block, author and founding CEO of Jean Block Consulting, Inc. (Albuquerque, NM). Drawing on decades of fundraising experience, Block shares five simple principles guaranteed to help nonprofits secure the resources they need and deserve.

1. **Remember the You:Me Ratio** — Fundraising is not about you and what you need; it's about the donor and what he needs in return for a gift. Review a solicitation letter for the number of YOUs versus MEs. Focus your writing and asking on the benefits to the donor, not the benefits to you.

2. **Ask for What You Want, or Take What You Get!** — Board volunteers are often not as successful as they could be because they are afraid to ask for a specific amount. Instead, they say "Can you help us?" or "Anything you can do would be greatly appreciated." Don't make a donor uncomfortable by making him/her name the amount. Ask for a specific amount and be ready to negotiate.

3. **Wait for the Person Who Can Say 'Yes'** — When contacting a potential funder, don't let the gatekeeper take your message or keep you from talking to the decision maker. Your energy, passion and enthusiasm can't be translated by someone else or captured on a while-you-were-out slip. If the potential funder isn't available, ask for voice mail and leave a message that you'll call back. Enthuse your message!

4. **Don't Be Afraid of 'No'** — "'No' can be the beginning of a long and fruitful conversation," Block says. "If you are told 'No,' first say 'Thank you! Thank you for taking my call and listening to my request.'" Then, ask these three questions:
   - ❑ "What do I need to know to ask better next time?
   - ❑ Now that you know who we are and what we offer, can you think of anyone else who might like to take advantage of this opportunity?
   - ❑ If you can't give money at this time, is there another way we might work together?"

5. **Thank, Thank, Thank** — Spend as much time, energy and creativity on thanking as you did asking. Make it timely and meaningful. Connect the donor with the results of his/her gift. Focus on outcomes. "If you don't have time to thank donors," Block says, "you shouldn't even ask."

*Source: Jean Block, President/CEO, Jean Block Consulting, Inc., Albuquerque, NM. Phone (505) 899-1520.*
*E-mail: jean@jblockinc.com. Website: http://www.jblockinc.com*

## It's Important to Nurture a Positive Attitude

Most sales performance problems are caused by lack of the right attitude rather than lack of sales skills. Potential is not truly effective unless it is driven by a winning attitude.

Here are steps to take to strengthen and maintain a positive attitude:

1. Take note of the total number of solicitation calls you make during the course of a week or month, not just the number of gifts or pledges you receive. It's been proven time and again that, on average, it takes a certain number of rejections before making a successful sale. Whatever that average is for you, accept it and take comfort in the fact that you're making contacts frequently and regularly. When you get discouraged, keep in mind: The more contacts you make, the better the odds of securing a gift!

2. Maintain a steady-as-she-goes point of view. Just as you should not get too caught up in a successful solicitation call, don't dwell on an unsuccessful attempt to secure a new gift. There are many external factors that impact giving, some of which we have no control over. Don't dwell on misfortune; move ahead.

3. Be enthusiastic about solicitation strategies brought to the table, old and new. Whether it's a new direct mail idea or an old solicitation strategy that was rejected a year ago, it may be just the approach your organization needs right now. Plus, when you greet all ideas enthusiastically, you encourage others to bring more ideas to you.

4. Look for good qualities in people, not negative ones. If you focus on positive aspects of colleagues, volunteers and prospects, your attitude will serve as a mirror in bringing out the best in others — whether it's greater productivity, a willingness to do more for your agency, or saying "yes" to your gift request. By stressing people's good points, you'll be taken more seriously by those with whom you come in contact. People tend to react positively to positive direction

## GETTING STARTED: BASIC FUNDRAISING STRATEGIES

## Determine If It's Time to Hire a Fundraising Consultant

These days, with nonprofit organizations simultaneously desperate to find revenue and making do with pared-down staffs, the question of whether to hire an outside fundraising consultant is a bit of a Catch-22: Can you afford to, with budgets stretched to the limits? Then again, can you really afford not to, with your work force stretched so thin?

Gail Meltzer, founding partner of CoreStrategies for Nonprofits (Miami, FL), a consulting firm for nonprofit organizations, shares a simple way to determine the need for a fundraising consultant: "Make a list of your fundraising goals and objectives for the next year and match the specific projects and tasks required for achieving those goals to your existing staff." Then ask yourself, "Do I already have on staff the time and skills required to meet my objectives?"

Still unsure whether it's time to hire an outside fundraising consultant? Meltzer shares some additional, yes-or-no questions that will help clarify your needs:

- ❑ Would hiring a consultant add credibility and urgency to our fundraising campaign or program? Would it galvanize our board?

- ❑ Would a consultant enable staff and volunteers to more successfully stay on task and on point?

- ❑ Do we need to resolve certain issues or challenges we're experiencing? Could an outside consultant provide a more efficient solution?

- ❑ Will a consultant enable us to move more quickly and efficiently through a project that is critical to other subsequent initiatives?

- ❑ Are we prepared to follow through on an outside consultant's recommendations?

- ❑ Once you have determined the need for a fundraising consultant, how can you maximize the value of hiring one?

Allen J. Proctor, founder of Allen Proctor Consulting (Worthington, OH) and author of "More Than Just Money: Practical and Provocative Steps to Nonprofit Success," says that the value in hiring a consultant should be measured by "the skill transfer to your staff members." For this reason, Proctor advises against hiring a consultant for a specific project, such as your first-ever fundraising gala.

"If you hire a consultant to do the work for you, your organization has not benefited from this person's skills," Proctor explains. Rather, hire a consultant when your goals are more conceptual: "If you want to increase last year's overall fundraising efforts by 50 percent, then hire a consultant," he says. The difference is, you're hiring someone to help you do your work better, not to do some one-time work for you.

Meltzer agrees that one of the best uses of a fundraising consultant isn't necessarily to plan a specific event, but to take advantage of the consultant's ability to think holistically, "Consultants can often create significant growth in organizations that know they need to change but have gotten stuck or stagnant, or worse, have begun a decline."

And perhaps most importantly, Meltzer says, a good fundraising consultant can provide something that your bare-bones staff may not have. "Fundraising consultants who keep themselves well-informed about changes in the field can bring a unique perspective to fund development staff who barely have time to think, let alone keep up with the changes that seem to occur almost daily."

*Sources: Gail S. Meltzer, Founding Partner, CoreStrategies for Nonprofits, Miami, FL. Phone (888) 458-4351.*
*E-mail: GailMeltzer@CoreStrategies4NonProfits.com.*
*Website: www.CoreStrategies4NonProfits.com*
*Allen J. Proctor, Founder, Allen Proctor Consulting, Worthington, OH. Phone: (614) 208-5403.*
*E-mail: proctorconsulting@columbus.rr.com.*
*Website: linkingmissiontomoney.com*

### How to Find a Consultant

"Referrals from colleagues at other nonprofits, whether staff or board members, is a great way to find out about effective consultants with proven track records," says Gail Meltzer, founding partner of CoreStrategies for Nonprofits (Miami, FL). Additionally, to find a fundraising consultant, Meltzer suggests the directories on the following websites:

- Association of Fundraising Professionals: http://consultants.afpnet.org

- Association for Healthcare Philanthropy: http://ahp.org/Pages/Home.aspx

- The Giving Institute: http://aafrc.org

- Partnership for Philanthropic Planning: http://www.pppnet.org/

- Nonprofit National Resource Directory: http://www.nonprofitnationalresourcedirectory.com/services

## Make Time to Review Systems and Policies

As you work to develop efficiencies that generate additional gift support, increase the number of contributors, enhance your organization's image and more, it's important to examine existing systems and policies to be sure they are efficient, effective and meeting stewardship goals.

Here are a few examples of systems and policies you should examine yearly:

- Gift acknowledgement process
- Filing system
- Gift acceptance policy and procedures
- Planned gifts policy
- Endowment policies
- Job descriptions and responsibilities
- Prospect research policy

- Organizational structure
- Volunteer structure and committees
- Board structure and committees
- Memorial gifts program
- Prospect tracking systems
- Campaign structure and process
- Existing marketing materials
- Pledge forms, letters of intent, etc.
- Gifts-in-kind policy
- Database management procedures
- Board and volunteer training
- Professional development
- Board and volunteer selection
- Hiring procedures

## Create Procedures for Addressing Mistakes

How should staff react when a donor calls and states his name was misspelled in the most recent annual report? What steps should be taken when a donor informs you an acknowledgement letter sent to her husband should have included her name as well?

It's human to make a mistake. When one does occur, however, it's wrong not to take corrective steps to minimize future mistakes.

Develop a step-by-step procedure such as this to correct mistakes and, as much as possible, prevent them from occurring in the first place:

1. When a mistake does occur, take immediate action to correct it. Go the extra mile.

2. Make the mistake a topic of discussion at your next staff meeting. Then arrive at a written solution to avoid similar mistakes in the future.

3. Finally, take preventative measures. Review existing programs and internal procedures to anticipate areas of vulnerability. Then take steps to minimize the possibility of future mistakes taking place.

# Fundraising Strategies for Small Shops

## PLANNING ACTIONS AND ANALYZING PERFORMANCE

*Planning and analysis are critical to successful fundraising. The former establishes the framework in which solicitation will be carried out; the latter defines the standards by which it will be reviewed, assessed and refined. Use the following resources to draft a comprehensive organizational plan and develop dependable procedures for analyzing performance.*

## Make Time to Develop an Annual Operational Plan

It's crucial to carry out thorough planning measures before jumping into a fundraising effort, especially if you're shooting for lofty goals.

A well-thought-out fundraising plan can break down those lofty goals into achievable components. Once yearly fundraising goals have been set, you're ready to begin mapping out a plan that will help achieve those goals.

Here is an example of steps to take to establish an annual operational plan:

1. **Set objectives** — Begin by coming up with a manageable number of quantifiable objectives that address overall goals. For example, if you have a yearly goal of raising $500,000 for your organization, you may have objectives that are similar to the following examples:

   - To secure $75,000 in $1,000-and-above gifts by fiscal year end.

   - To secure $40,000 in direct mail revenue by fiscal year end.

   - To secure $150,000 in phonathon gifts by fiscal year end.

   - To secure $40,000 through special fundraisers.

   - To secure $125,000 in corporate/foundation support by fiscal year end.

   - To secure $70,000 in new gifts from individuals and/or businesses.

2. **Create action plans** — Once quantifiable objectives are set, formulate action plans that address how you intend to meet each objective. Action plans may outline special fundraising projects such as a special event or series of direct mail appeals or a phonathon. Collectively, the sum of each action plan will be equal to that total for a particular objective. Here are examples of action plans that address securing $75,000 in $1,000-and-above gifts by fiscal year end:

   - Make personal calls on all donors who gave at the $1,000-plus level last year, inviting them to renew (or increase) giving for this fiscal year.

   - Host a president's reception to which all of last year's $1,000-plus contributors are invited and urged to bring a prospective donor who could give at that level.

   - Charge the development committee with responsibility for securing 10 or more new $1,000-plus gifts by year end.

   Although the above listed examples would require more detail — explaining what needs to happen when and who's in charge — you can see how each strategy supports how that particular objective will be achieved.

3. **Develop a master calendar** — After all fundraising strategies for each objective have been spelled out through action plans, it's time to assemble a master timetable or calendar that includes the target date for every strategy and action plan component — everything from production schedules for printed communications to phonathon planning schedules and so forth.

| Operational Plan Components | |
| --- | --- |
| **Goals:** | More lofty — set the direction of the department or organization. |
| **Objectives:** | Quantifiable, more narrow — support the organization's goals. |
| **Action plans:** | Spell out how each quantifiable objective will be attained. |
| **Master calendar:** | Chronological dates of who does what and by when; highly detailed. |

## Develop a Yearlong Plan for Soliciting Nondonors

Do you have a plan in place that outlines strategies for converting nondonors into contributors? Although retention of past donors should be a top priority in any operational plan, it's also important to keep expanding your base of annual support.

As you create a yearlong plan of strategies aimed at converting nondonors, here are some examples you may want to include:

- List the names of nondonors you would most like to see on next year's list of contributors.

- Share your nondonor list with your volunteer or board development committee monthly or quarterly, encouraging members to develop solicitation strategies for each person or business.

- Develop a yearlong series of direct-mail appeals targeted at your nondonor list. Have one or more specific funding projects in mind. Offer special benefits/incentives for first-time givers.

- Coordinate a special event that reaches out to new prospects and provides a forum to educate the public on your mission and programs.

- Develop fundraising strategies targeting specific nondonor groups — e.g., physicians, professional women — that make sense for your nonprofit.

- Instruct staff to make a minimum number of calls on nondonors each week or month.

- Secure a challenge gift directed to matching any gifts from new donors over a specified period of time.

- Coordinate a telesolicitation effort using volunteers or paid callers with nondonors as its focus.

- Host a series of on-site receptions with donors hosting nondonors.

These and other strategies will help broaden your source of annual gift support.

## How to Create Your Fundraising Plan

When planning fundraising strategies for your new fiscal year, one of the first steps is to analyze the strengths and weaknesses of the previous year.

"Successful planning requires a focus on the overall goal and the ability to examine strategies objectively, without taking it personally when pet projects or ideas don't make the plan," says Michele Van Dyke, executive director, Luverne Area Community Foundation (Luverne, MN). "Remember strategies wear out just like clothes and need to be replaced with something new regularly."

To build your strategic fundraising plan, Van Dyke suggests inviting staff and board members to an all-day retreat away from your worksite. Options to consider include hiring an independent facilitator or board member with similar skills to help the group stick to the goal and time constraints of the day. Prior to the event, write a focused agenda with timeframes and distribute to all who will attend. Provide everyone with long-range strategy information and plans from previous years.

Van Dyke advises to begin by reviewing your strategic plan from the previous year and discussing the actual outcomes. She feels that is a great way to identify potential for growth and improvement. Stick to timeframes and bring all suggestions back to the office where the strategic plan can be assembled, complete with work plans. If applicable, let each department develop its work plan around its goals and objectives.

As the year progresses, review progress towards goals and objectives monthly and update board members quarterly. Informed board members are better able to communicate your successes to the community. To bring in a continual supply of new ideas each year, Van Dyke says, find a group of great volunteers and board members, and change membership periodically to stay fresh.

*Source: Michele Van Dyke, Executive Director, Luverne Area Community Foundation, Luverne, MN.*
*Phone (507) 220-2424. E-mail: vandykem@sanfordhealth.org*

## Set Goal to Increase Participation Rate

Having a high percentage of your constituency contributing annually benefits your organization beyond the bottom line by adding credibility to your case when seeking grants and increasing the likelihood of securing more major gifts.

To increase your number of contributors by a specific percentage:

1. Based on your constituency size, determine how many additional contributors are needed to increase donor participation by a certain percentage (e.g., 5 or 10 percent).

2. Draft a plan — including direct mail, telesolicitation and face-to-face solicitation strategies — to boost your giving units by that percentage.

This may sound simple, but many organizations have no plan in place to increase their donor participation rates. Make your organization the exception — then work to win exceptional gifts.

## Calendar Keeps Fundraising on Track

Shelby Anderson, associate director of field fundraising, and Jennifer Legere, director of field fundraising, of MADD National Office (Irving, TX), wanted a way to keep development officers at local offices on track with fundraising, so they gave them the necessary tools.

They created a cultivation calendar:

- Each month has different tips and tasks to perform to keep in contact with potential donors.

- The supporters are ranked from A to C; A indicates the highest level of support, B indicates the middle and C indicates support on a smaller level.

- To keep in contact, chapters are encouraged to call, e-mail and visit potential supporters in person. The calendar lets them know when communication should happen and who should do it.

## Looking Beyond the Dollars

Financial objectives address gift dollars to be raised, but non-monetary objectives help focus fundraising processes and systems, says Patti Lyons, executive partner at Pride Philanthropy (Alpharetta, GA).

The metrics Lyons identifies, many of which can help board members strengthen fundraising efforts, include:

- Percent of constituency contributing during the year
- Percent of constituency solicited by mail, as well as face-to-face
- Average gift size
- Number of new donors over prior year
- Percent of new donors over prior year
- Percent of pledges paid
- Number of volunteers from year to year
- Number of major gift prospects

- For example, in one week e-mails should be sent to all of the C companies, an A company should get a personal visit by a board member and faxes should go out to all companies.

Anderson says the calendars really work and Legere says the proof is in the pudding, so to speak. Strong fundraising staffs really take advantage of the calendar and follow it.

Anderson and Legere have collected the calendar tips themselves over the years. They also encourage chapters to take mental notes about each company to personalize the fundraising potential and include these notes on their calendars.

*Source: Shelby Anderson, Associate Director of Field Fundraising, Jennifer Legere, Director of Field Fundraising, MADD National Office, Irving, TX. Phone (469) 420-4580. E-mail: Shelby.Anderson@madd.org*

- Number of planned gifts
- Number of planned gift expectancies
- Number of gifts matched by employers
- Number of donors moving to higher levels
- Number of new members
- Number of event attendees
- Cost ratios for each special event
- Percent of successful grant applications
- Number of corrected addresses
- Number of renewed lapsed donors
- Percent of previous year's donors
- Number of board calls and/or referrals

*Source: Patti Lyons, Executive Partner, Pride Philanthropy, Alpharetta, GA. Phone (888) 417-0707. E-mail: Pattilyons@aol.com Website: www.pridephilanthropy.com*

## Make To-do Lists a Part of Your Everyday Routine

Do you get bogged down putting out daily brushfires only to find out by day's end that little of what you had initially hoped to accomplish got any of your attention?

This can easily happen to anyone involved with fundraising, especially if priorities aren't clearly set in advance.

If you haven't already done so, get into the habit of making a daily to-do list that includes appointments and those projects that you deem as highest priority. Some people make their to-do lists at the end of the previous day (so they can come to work and hit the ground running). Others choose to make that the first item of business each day.

Whatever method you use (Outlook, some other software, a digital voice recorder or a simple 3 X 5-inch note card), and whatever time of day you choose to do it, get into the daily habit of making a to-do list.

> To-do List — April 13, 2011
> 8:15:  Staff mtg.
>
> 10:30:  Meet w/Doris Osborne, President, Osborne, Inc.
>
> 12:00:  Lunch w/board member Elmer Lindstrom
>
> _____  Set three appointments for next week
>
> _____  Finish Hartwell proposal
>
> _____  Update prospect tracking summary

## Analyze Mid-year Giving Stats

Halfway through your fiscal year, take time to analyze where annual giving stands in relation to your year-end goal. Then take steps to ensure your annual fund goal will be met and even surpassed.

Here's some of what you can do during this mid-year check up:

✓ Identify lybunts (those who gave last year but not this). Who's on this list, especially among higher giving levels? Recognizing it's far easier to retain a donor than to acquire a new one, make a concerted effort to approach them and get them back on board.

✓ Approach those persons who generally give the last half of your fiscal year. Why wait until later to discover who intends to give and who doesn't?

✓ Have someone establish a challenge gift to match all new and increased gifts between now and the end of your year.

✓ Involve your loyal higher-end donors in identifying and accompanying you on calls to nondonors capable of making gifts of $1,000 and above.

## Calculate Time Invested Against Total Dollar Returns

As you map out your fundraising year and create an operational plan complete with goals, objectives, action plans and timeline, it's helpful to analyze the time invested in each fundraising strategy against the dollar return for that effort. If, for instance, you discover that a direct mail appeal you sent out took minimal time but produced a significant return, you may decide to increase direct mail appeals in the upcoming year instead of spending time on a labor-intensive special event that had a marginal return.

Although there are other factors one needs to evaluate when planning upcoming development strategies (e.g., project costs, etc.), time is a key issue based on limited development personnel. And while it may be challenging to estimate the time required to carry out a particular fundraising strategy from beginning to end, you will no doubt be able to calculate invested time to a reasonable degree. The key is to be consistent in the way in which you arrive at calculations — whether your are including support staff time, etc.

The chart below helps to illustrate how you might analyze each fundraising effort's invested time against its dollar return.

Content not available in this edition

# Fundraising Strategies for Small Shops

## MAKING THE MOST OF FACE-TO-FACE SOLICITATION

*Face-to-face solicitation is the bedrock of all effective fundraising. Though technology has given the fundraiser many new tools, nothing can take the place of looking a donor in the eye and discussing cherished hopes and aspirations. The prospect of personal solicitation can be intimidating, but understanding a few foundational principles will greatly enhance your comfort and success with this important type of fundraising.*

## The Case Statement: Selling Your Vision to Donor Prospects

Behavioral research shows that donors are fundamentally skeptical about donating to nonprofits, says Tom Ahern, author and principle of Ahern Communications, Ink (Foster, RI). "The most ancient parts of our brain are concerned only with survival," he says, "and they need a very compelling reason to part with hard-earned money."

A concise and compelling case statement is key to providing this reason, Ahern says. Here, he discusses some of the fine points of this important solicitation tool:

### *What is the bedrock of a successful case statement?*

"Everything in a good case statement is focused on answering three key questions: 'Why this organization?' 'Why now?' and 'Why should I care?'. You need to explain why your project is uniquely valuable and more worthy of investment than other projects. You need to explain why the donor should write a check today instead of next week or next year. And you need to explain why the donor should care about what your vision is and what you are trying to do."

### *How should a case statement be used? What is it designed to do?*

"A case statement is a tool to be used in face-to-face solicitation. You don't send it to the prospect in advance, you bring it with you to the meeting. You have it in your hands to prompt the points you want to focus on, and you might open it up at times to illustrate a point or have the prospect look at something. When the meeting is over, the case statement can also be left with the prospect as he or she is considering a gift."

### *What does a good case statement look like? Pages of text? A short list of bullet points?*

"There is no formulaic answer, but in general you want to make the statement as short as possible (see related story, bottom right). The core case for Yale's $3.2 billion Yale Tomorrow campaign was only 550 words. The rest of the document was pages and pages of photographs and provocative quotes about how uncertain the world can be and how important it is to plan for the future."

### *What kinds of facts should a case statement include?*

"There are two basic types of evidence: statistical and anecdotal. Research shows that donors respond far more strongly to one anecdote about one person than to any amount of statistics. Stats should be used, but as a background that reinforces the central narrative. It's also important to know that research has shown people respond much more strongly to the story of a single child than the story of that child and a sibling. Adding even one other person to an anecdote makes it less effective, and adding more than that just crushes donor response."

### *What is the biggest misconception nonprofits have about making their case with prospects?*

"Talking too much about themselves. People don't give to charities, they give through them. Unfortunately, charities forget they're only a means for a donor to help solve a problem. I've seen case statements asking for $150 million in which the donor is never mentioned, the word 'you' is never used. That is not an engaging practice and not a good way to get support."

*Source: Tom Ahern, Principle, Ahern Communications, Ink, Foster, RI. Phone (401) 397-8104. E-mail: A2Bmail@aol.com*

---

### Short, Shorter, Even Shorter Yet

Tom Ahern, principle of Ahern Communications, Ink (Foster, RI), has a story about the importance of ruthless brevity in compelling case statements:

A college developed a 2,500-word statement for an upcoming campaign and started approaching top supporters with it. One prospect looked at the lengthy statement, scratched his head, and after several minutes of explanation, asked if the campaign could be boiled down to the aim of furthering academic excellence. When the gift officer said it could, the man said, "Well I support academic excellence. How much are you looking for today?"

Don't over-complicate the solicitation process, Ahern says. "You need to get the heart of your entire vision across in the first 30 to 50 words. You need to be able to express your central aim in just a sentence or two. And if you can't do that, you probably don't really understand what you are doing and why."

---

## MAKING THE MOST OF FACE-TO-FACE SOLICITATION

### Choose Words Carefully to Further Your Major Gift Efforts

The words you choose can have a major impact on the outcome of your major gift solicitation, says Martin Leifeld, vice chancellor of university advancement at the University of Missouri-St. Louis (St. Louis, MO).

"Words and phrasing of questions are very important," Leifeld says. "(The words) 'We need your help,' will not get the job done very often. 'We can help each other advance something we're both passionate about,' has a much better chance of success."

Leifeld shares examples of wording he uses in typical solicitation situations:

*When laying groundwork in a feeling-out call...*

"For any university to move from level to level, significant investments are required from alumni. A successful alumnus like you knows, by virtue of the people you chat with in the boardroom and the executive suite, that your peers are making significant gifts to their alma maters. We need a similar level of leadership for this institution to remain competitive. Now you have been very successful at XYZ Corporation, and it is leaders just like you that can enable institutions like ours to make great strides forward."

Thoughtful silence following mention of a large gift is common, says Leifield. Though such silence gives little concrete feedback, it means the prospect is internalizing what you are saying and is, therefore, a positive sign.

*After a prospect balks at a large dollar request...*

"I understand it's a lot to consider, but I'm not asking for a commitment today. What I would like to ask you to think about, though, is this: Would you give at that level if you could? If you could find a way to do so, would supporting the university at that level of generosity be something you would like to pursue?"

This question moves prospects from thinking about what they can do to the much more productive question of what they would like to do, say Leifeld. Large numbers always have a place in the solicitation experience, even if they don't materialize, he says. "Even when people come in below the request amount, they never forget that there is an expectation for alumni of means to show leadership. It works on them over time."

*At the conclusion of a meeting establishing general gift parameters...*

"I'm feeling very positive about what we've accomplished today. When we get together next time, I'd like to meet in your office, so we can close the door and focus on the details of what we can do together."

Leifeld says shaping prospects' expectations of future encounters helps them prepare mentally and emotionally while making for more focused and productive meetings.

*If a prospect says he/she needs time to consider a solicitation...*

"I completely understand. Would two weeks be enough time? Or do you think you would need three?"

Leifield says scheduling the next step in the process is crucial in maintaining a sense of forward momentum and keeping your gift request (and not someone else's) at the forefront of a prospect's mind.

*Source: Martin Leifeld, Vice Chancellor of University Advancement, University of Missouri-St. Louis, St. Louis, MO. Phone (314) 516-4278. E-mail: leifeldm@umsl.edu*

---

#### Bring Right Tone to Gift Solicitations

Confidence, urgency and optimism can all strike a chord with potential donors, but one shade of emotion stands out above them all, says Martin Leifeld, vice chancellor of university advancement at the University of Missouri-St. Louis (St. Louis, MO):

"I find having a certain gravitas in the room — like one is taking part in a very ennobling experience — is very effective. When donors reach a sober and considered conclusion in an atmosphere of seriousness, the experience can be amazingly powerful."

---

### Factors to Consider When Setting Initial Ask Amounts

At what level should you ask those folks who have never contributed to your organization to give?

Before making that decision, Jason Fisher, senior counsel, Advancement Solutions Consulting (Cedar Rapids, IA), recommends asking these three key questions:

1. **What does the average graduate make in salary after leaving your school?** Conventional wisdom suggests that schools with a history of producing higher-salary graduates can start at a higher amount.
2. **What does your average donor currently give?**
3. **What gift club levels does your organization currently offer?** Fisher says some people just like being part of a club. Your staff can use established club levels to justify starting the ask at a certain dollar amount.

The most important factor to remember when setting levels, Fisher says, is to not underestimate your prospects' giving potential. "The vast majority of never givers choose not to give because of their lack of interest, not their financial ability."

*Source: Jason Fisher, Senior Counsel, Advancement Solutions Consulting, A Division of RuffaloCODY, Cedar Rapids, IA. Phone (319) 892-0376. E-mail: Jason.Fisher@ruffalocody.com*

## Avoid the Premature Ask

While many fundraising professionals experience call reluctance — the fear of asking for gifts — asking prematurely for what could have been a major gift is also a common problem.

Recognize that you may be asking for a gift too soon if the prospect:

- Continues to avoid repeated attempts to discuss the issue.

- Responds by saying he/she is far more involved with charities other than yours.

- Makes a token gift or pledge you consider to be far less than the prospect is capable of giving.

- Seems indifferent to the funding opportunities you have shared.

## Select From Among Various Presentation Formats

If making calls on prospective and existing donors is a part of your responsibilities, your effectiveness will improve significantly if you develop and practice presentations with different objectives in mind. Knowing in advance what to say and how to direct the conversation during an often brief encounter can positively impact solicitation success.

By developing and selecting from a menu of presentation outlines prior to each call, you can speak with greater confidence because objectives have been identified and you have a plan as to how your 20-minute conversation will progress.

This flash card approach to call preparation serves as a useful tool as you prepare to meet with numerous prospects and donors at various points in the solicitation cycle.

You can develop three or four basic outlines to use as pre-call guides. Or you can build a wide assortment of presentation approaches on which to rely, depending on the prospect/donor type (e.g., business, individual, first-time call, past donor) and each call's objective (e.g., to solicit a gift, introduce your charity, or cultivate a relationship).

First, list the various types of calls you make — introductory, solicitation, stewardship, cultivation, etc. Then review the list and decide which most-used approaches would be improved by developing a presentation outline.

Prior to making each call, pull out the appropriate flash card to review your objective and key points you will want to cover. You may choose to add more detail to a particular outline as you customize it for a particular prospect.

This quick review will put you on track for accomplishing your goals and help you develop various presentation styles for different circumstances.

Create several presentation scenarios, then test them after some practice. Doing so will help to design a method that works best for you. You will no doubt reach the day when the flash card approach is no longer necessary, but until that time, this technique helps to formulate a methodical approach to individual calls.

---

**Objective**
Introduce our cause and measure level of interest.

**Prospect Type**
Business/New prospect

*Presentation Sequence* ——

1. Ask probing questions that give insight into prospect's ability/inclination to give.
2. Link prospect's response in some way to charity's mission/purpose.
3. Demonstrate how charity is addressing its mission locally/regionally.
4. Share examples of charity's economic impact on community/region.
5. Share examples of how others' gifts have made accomplishments possible.
6. [...] to support the charity's efforts.
7. [...]

---

**Objective**
Information gathering: funding interests/past giving

**Prospect Type**
Individual/Past Donor

*Presentation Sequence* ——

1. Share summary of charity's strategic plan.
2. Ask for honest input/response to plan.
3. Ask which elements of plan most excite/interest donor.
4. Seek answers that measure prospect's interest in certain components.
5. Invite the donor to "dream." How would he/she visualize the realization of particular long-range plans?
6. Explain how you plan to utilize the donor's input.
7. Agree to next meeting to follow up on the donor's advice/input.

---

**Objective**
Solicit increased annual gift (President's Club).

**Prospect Type**
Business/Past Donor (Under $1,000)

*Presentation Sequence* ——

1. Recognize the donor's past history of loyal support.
2. Point to charity's accomplishments as a result of gift support.
3. Delineate charity's plans for future/greater achievements.
4. Identify funding projects of interest to donor.
5. Build the case for increased support.
6. Invite to join the President's Club (gift of $1,000 or more).
7. Agree on how/when a gift will be made or other follow-up.

## Make Donor Calls a Valued Experience

Do the donors and donor prospects on whom you call look forward to your annual or semi-annual visit? Would they miss you — or even notice — if you stopped calling?

As you complete call reports after face-to-face visits, evaluate and record the mood of your visit. Was the prospect/donor attentive, interested and pleased to see you? Your sense of the prospect's level of interest and enthusiasm will alert you to changes that might be made for future visits.

Remember that your level of enthusiasm will have the single greatest impact on the donor's attentiveness to your presentation. To keep these annual calls interesting and informative — and something people look forward to each year —vary your presentation from year to year by incorporating any of the following techniques:

- Bring a board member along to express appreciation for past gifts and encourage increased giving.

- Share a news clipping related to the donor's business to show interest in his/her work.

- Invite a client served by your organization (e.g. student, former patient, youth, etc.) to accompany you on the call and express appreciation. If it's not possible to bring along a client, hand the donor a personal note of appreciation written by one.

- Impart some real examples of how your charity is making a positive difference in the community or region.

- Survey your donor to seek his/her opinion or advice on matters related to your cause.

- Share a visual summary (e.g., flip chart, video, etc.) of your strategic plans or feasibility study results that provides insider information on your organization's future.

## Get to 'Yes' Through Solicitation Scripting and Rehearsal

Have a sizable gift solicitation on the horizon? You might want to start practicing now, says Martin Leifeld, vice chancellor of university advancement at the University of Missouri–St. Louis (St. Louis, MO).

"Major gift solicitations can and should be well-scripted in advance," says Leifeld, who regularly rehearses his solicitations of prospective donors with staff members to the point of hammering out even the language he will use and the questions he will ask.

Scripting and rehearsal can improve many aspects of the solicitation process, says Leifeld. Among the areas he highlights are:

- ❑ **Relationships**. Finding people well-matched to a prospect's status, personality and interests is a vital part of the solicitation process, says Leifeld. Scripting a call in advance ensures that the right people will be in the room and that nondevelopment participants are prepared for the role(s) they will play.

- ❑ **Comfort level**. Development professionals get nervous no matter how many years are under their belt, says Leifeld. Prior rehearsal is what helps them move through any hesitation they might experience.

- ❑ **Tough questions**. Major solicitations often include questions that must be asked but which will create a certain amount of discomfort. Practicing these questions ahead of time and deciding which team member will ask them helps ensure they are not omitted, says Leifeld.

- ❑ **Varied responses**. "A donor will either agree to the gift, ask for time to consider, suggest a lower gift amount or decline," says Leifeld. Preparing strategies appropriate

to each of these donor responses is key to effective solicitation.

- ❑ **Contingency plans**. The CEO of a major corporation once declined Leifeld's primary and back-up opportunities, and asked what else he had to offer. Luckily, says Leifeld, he and his team had talked through a number of projects before the meeting, and the CEO loved the third project they pitched.

To ensure development officers are adequately prepared, Leifeld asks them to fill out a short meeting summary form (shown below) before making solicitation calls. He says the worksheet provides a simple way to review fundraising basics such as donor giving history while getting staff thinking about meeting strategy and approach ahead of time.

*Source: Martin Leifeld, Vice Chancellor of University Advancement, University of Missouri–St. Louis, St. Louis, MO. Phone (314) 516-4278. E-mail: leifeldm@umsl.edu*

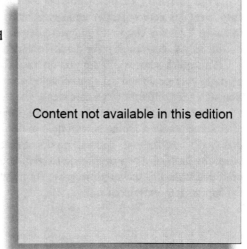

Content not available in this edition

# Fundraising Strategies for Small Shops

## BUILDING A ROBUST ANNUAL FUND

*In many nonprofits, the annual fund is the primary source of financial support. The fund provides operating revenue and meets costs — ongoing programs, employee compensation, administrative overhead — that donors might otherwise be reluctant to support. Augmenting this critical aspect of your fundraising program with the following strategies and approaches will pay dividends for years to come.*

## 12 Reasons Why $25 Gifts are Important

So much emphasis is placed on major gifts that one begins to wonder if any effort should be put into securing smaller gifts, say for $25.

Clearly, every fundraising or operational plan should include strategies directed toward securing such gifts. That doesn't mean time allocated to major gifts should take a back seat, but it does mean smaller gifts play an important role in the overall fundraising plan.

Here are 12 reasons why $25 gifts are important:

1. Most major gifts come from those who previously made smaller gifts.

2. Since word-of-mouth from a loyal donor is oftentimes a nonprofit's best sales tool, it pays to have as many current donors as possible, regardless of gift size.

3. Converting 1,000 nondonors into $25 donors results in $25,000 in new gifts, an increase that most development offices would cherish.

4. A gift of $25 from a new prospect moves him/her into your membership or giving club pipeline. Benefits at each gift level should encourage him/her to increase giving over time.

5. Increasing the percentage of constituency giving — among your community, your employees, your alumni, etc. — provides a degree of leverage when approaching foundations for support. "Ninety-seven percent of our employees contribute and 77 percent of our community's businesses give annually."

6. Once someone contributes to your school or nonprofit, he/she has identified him/herself as one who believes in and supports your work. You can then take steps to cultivate that relationship further.

7. Although there are many exceptions, most planned gifts result from those who have given previously.

8. Oftentimes the person who makes a smaller gift may be making more of a sacrificial gift (based on his/her income) than one who contributes at a higher level but could afford to do much more. And sacrificial donors — those who give to the best of their ability — are among your most loyal ambassadors.

9. Your published annual list of contributors serves as a testimonial to others who have yet to contribute.

10. Contributors often become involved in some volunteer capacity.

11. You cannot build a habit of giving without receiving that first gift, regardless of its size.

12. Both the donor and those served by the charity benefit whenever a gift of any size is made.

Major gifts — and the time devoted to their identification, research, cultivation, solicitation and stewardship — are important. But don't interpret that as a dictate to overlook approaches aimed at encouraging gifts at all levels.

## Synchronize Fundraising With Yearly Giving Cycles

Looking to boost the revenue of a critical annual fundraiser or donor appeal? Take a hard look at your calendar, says Sarayl Shunkamolah, associate director of annual giving at The University of Montana Foundation (Missoula, MT).

"Our fundraising is heavily weighted toward the fall semester because reliable donors tend to give at the beginning of every academic year," Shunkamolah says. "Our phonathon runs for 12 weeks in the fall and 12 weeks in the spring, but because of the difference in donor giving patterns, we are targeting $225,000 in the fall this year and only $60,000 in the spring."

Staff also target past donors in fall and new and lapsed donors in spring.

*Source: Sarayl Shunkamolah, Associate Director of Annual Giving, The University of Montana Foundation, Missoula, MT. Phone (406) 243-2593. E-mail:Sarayl.Shunkamolah@mso.umt.edu*

## Weigh Organization-specific Factors to Set Annual Fund Goal

*Q. How do you set annual fund goals?*

"It depends. Annual giving goals are set in many ways depending on the culture and needs of each institution. Sometimes I have been handed a goal for unrestricted giving that equals the amount necessary to balance the budget. Other times it has been a figure negotiated with volunteer class leaders integral to the fundraising effort. I feel in the best cases that the annual giving goal is a combination of unrestricted and budget-relieving designations that is reflective of many areas of input, such as financial aid, program support and faculty support. These requests are then balanced against the reality of what can be raised. Surprisingly, young, underdeveloped programs can actually apply a higher percentage of growth than most fully developed programs. The dollars are clearly different, however. When setting annual fund goals, be sure to factor in key items such as real strong reunion classes and weak reunion classes, and one-time anomaly gifts. The longer your historical record, the closer you can come to accurate projections."

— *Ken Goebel, Director of Development, Keene State College (Keene, NH)*

"I used to go to great lengths to determine a goal with complex methodology before finally settling on a simple five-percent increase in dollars and donors every year. Simpler is better. However, this will depend on the maturity of your program. Less mature programs, with a leadership change or automation of their call center, will see increases greater than this in a given year. When speaking with your leadership about your annual giving goal, keep fairness in mind. Your annual giving goal should never be a greater percentage increase than the major gift goal. Your major giving staff shouldn't be provided with a five percent increase as a goal and the annual giving staff a 50 percent increase as a goal."

— *Michael Westfall, Vice President, Eastern Washington University Foundation (Cheney, WA)*

## Three Changes That Could Boost Your Annual Appeal

Looking to pump up results for your annual appeal? So were officials at Lawrence University (Appleton, WI). And they're finding success doing so with three simple changes, says Ben Campbell, associate director of annual giving.

Campbell shares the three techniques they have recently added to breathe new life into their annual fundraising program:

- **Communicate via e-mail.** Campbell says he is testing a new idea with a small number of class agents where they send out an e-mail to their classmates, in addition to the regular letters and calls they make. He says agents were encouraged to make the e-mail positive and personal, while sharing some numbers about the current state of the campaign (e.g., number of new donors, total amount raised by their specific class, etc.).
- **Send an early-bird mailing.** Sent at the beginning of the next fiscal year, this encourages giving early and gives a jump-start to your campaign. In Lawrence University's case, Campbell says, this mailing grabs people's attention because of its unexpected timing, since traditionally, the first appeal wasn't sent until the third month of the fiscal year.
- **Switch appeal order.** Campbell says they have five main direct mail appeals each year. Two of them are class agent mailings, which have the strongest returns because alumni tend to respond to their classmates' ask better. These used to be the second and third appeals, but are now the second (behind only the new early-bird mailing) and fifth to maximize the opportunity to receive gifts early in the fiscal year and act as a catch-all at the end.

*Source: Benjamin C. Campbell, Associate Director of Annual Giving, Lawrence University, Appleton, WI. Phone (920) 832-6936. E-mail: benjamin.c.campbell@lawrence.edu*

## To Better Target Prospects, Segment Your List

People contribute based on their interests. To appeal to their interests, it's important that you segment your list.

Whether you are creating direct mail appeals or coordinating a phonathon effort, targeting segmented groups will increase your gift response rate.

Make time to analyze your existing constituency list and prioritize segmentation opportunities that can be tested throughout the year.

Here are a few segmentation examples:

- Married with no children
- Place of residence (ZIP code)
- Avocation
- Family-owned businesses
- Widows/widowers
- People with second residences

- Occupation
- Gender, race, religion
- Age
- Political interests
- Art collection owners
- Land rich individuals

Explore the possibilities, then match various groups with giving opportunities.

## Annual Fund Handouts Should Help Close the Sale

When seeking annual fund support, it's important to leave prospects with a handout that furthers your invitation to invest in your cause and that your prospect wants to hang onto and not toss the minute you are out the door. To make your handout more compelling:

1. **Know that the design matters.** Even though the brochure's message is far more important than its look, the design can help capture the prospect's attention. Create a visually appealing piece laid out in a way that will invite them to read on.

2. **Refer to the piece during your presentation.** You need not walk through every component of the brochure, but referring to key points will add credibility to the handout's value.

3. **Show would-be donors what's in it for them.** As compelling as your message may be, it won't matter if the prospective donor doesn't see what's in it for him/her.

4. **Make your call to action explicit and obvious.** Even if you offer the prospect giving options, there should be no question about what it is you expect of them.

5. **Make it easy as pie to respond.** Include a pledge card and return envelope. Include complete contact information for you and people within your office with direct phone numbers and e-mail addresses.

---

### Employ New Approaches for Annual Fund Brochures

Developing annual fund literature for a new fiscal year? Looking for new ways to make a compelling case for annual support? Consider:

1. **Incorporating testimonials.** Testimonials (from those served by your organization, board members, staff, donors, community leaders and others) provide a powerful reason to make annual contributions.

2. **Tying annual support to long-range plans.** Summarize key elements of your nonprofit's strategic plans. Show how increased annual giving is necessary to expand future services.

3. **Zeroing in on your mission.** Focus on the lifeblood relationship between annual gifts and mission fulfillment.

4. **Providing a menu of annual gift opportunities.** Share specific needs. Offer choices of gift opportunities and ranges of gifts.

5. **Demonstrating the accomplishments of last year's annual fund.** Show donors how last year's support made a noticeable difference. Then make the case for this year's effort.

6. **Emphasizing benefits the donor receives.** Point out how the donor will benefit — directly or indirectly — by giving to your annual giving campaign (e.g., tax deduction, member benefits, etc.).

7. **Concentrating on the human element.** Focus on one individual who has benefited from your services, or do a day-in-the-life story of three or four persons served by your nonprofit.

---

## Keep Donors Coming Back

So you've managed to get that first gift from a new donor. Whether it's a major gift or a small offering to your annual campaign, your primary consideration should be retaining that donor so he/she continues to support your cause.

To keep donors engaged and interested in giving to your cause in the long run:

✓ **Know your donor as a person.** You have heard that friendship should precede love. The same holds true in donor development. Get to know donors as people first. What do they like? What are their interests? What drew them to your organization? Where do they work? Asking these questions will lead to a genuine relationship that will strongly resonate with any donor.

✓ **Keep the relationship mutual.** Make sure the relationship works for both parties. What does your donor need? Whom do you know who can help with that need? Connecting donors through networking opportunities is a great way to say thanks for their support.

✓ **Follow their lead.** Donor policies should not be one-size-fits-all. It's imperative to know what your donors want. Knowing this will keep you from mailing to them too often, sending them things they don't want and asking for amounts they can't give.

✓ **Give them the credit.** In publications, mailings and on your website, keep donors front and center. Tell people your work wouldn't be possible without donors. Tell stories of individual donors who have stretched a bit to make a larger gift or who made a personal connection with one of the people you serve. Putting donors first tells them they are vital to your mission.

## Turn to a Backup Plan When Your Annual Goal Is in Doubt

As you prepare your annual fundraising operational plan, map out a backup plan with fundraising strategies you can implement immediately should the possibility of reaching your yearly goal become questionable.

If, for instance, your fiscal year began in July and in January you find that you're shy of where you need to be, put that backup plan in place.

What strategies could your backup plan include? Although strategic elements will vary greatly from organization to organization, some examples include:

✓ Announcing a compelling mid-year funding project that will draw support from both existing donors and those persons who have yet to support your annual effort.

✓ Coordinating a fresh special event that was not a part of your original operational plan.

✓ Enlisting board members and others to call on lybunts and sybunts — those who gave last year (or in some years) but not this year.

✓ Convincing a donor to establish a mid-year challenge gift that will match all new and increased gifts for the remainder of your fiscal year.

✓ Approaching businesses to sponsor particular programs or events as opposed to asking for outright gifts.

## Use Mini Capital Campaign To Re-engage Lapsed Donors

 ***What's your strategy to reach lapsed donors of five to 10 years?***

"Many institutions treat donors who have been lapsed for this length of time like nondonors, then are surprised when they are unable to reacquire their support.

"I recommend you treat lapsed donors of five to 10 years like a mini-capital campaign. Use a pre-approach letter to thank them for previous support and ask them to renew, use specific initiatives that will be either directly or indirectly funded through the annual fund as case points, get a current donor to sponsor a renewal challenge and use students to make the calls.

"The last time I used this approach we generated a 25 percent pledge rate with an average gift of $79. Ask amounts were tailored to the last gift and the length of time they had been lapsed. Callers were specifically assigned and trained to address the gaps in giving, using phrases like: 'Thank you for your previous support, we're sorry we've not kept in better touch.'"

— *Darian Litif, Associate Director of New Business, DCM (Brooklyn, NY)*

# Fundraising Strategies for Small Shops

## PROMOTING MAJOR GIFTS AND PLANNED GIVING

*In terms of cost per dollar raised, major gifts and planned giving are an extremely efficient form of fundraising. Not only do they involve large-dollar donations, they involve close and personal relationships with donors, greatly increasing the likelihood of future gifts. Whether your organization's major gift threshold is $1,000 or $100,000, the following strategies will help you identify and acquire the transformational donations your organization needs.*

## Be Careful Not to Make Assumptions About Major Gift Donors

When it comes to attracting major gift donors, could you be laboring under the false assumption that all major-gift minds think alike? Doing so could ultimately work against you.

"Motivation patterns differ according to individuals, age of donors, levels of major-gift giving, etc.," says Veronique Diriker, director of development at the University of Maryland Eastern Shore (Princess Anne, MD).

When working with major donors, Diriker says, here are some key stereotypes you should avoid:

1. **That all donors want tangible publicity benefits, such as name plaques.** "This is mostly true for corporations but untrue for individuals," says Diriker. Bring up the subject of naming gently during your discussions. It should be easy to tell based on the donor's reaction just how interested he or she is.

2. **That glossy brochures and pamphlets, or an elaborate multimedia pitch, are needed to make donors believe in your cause.** "Personal contact is key," Diriker says, and will always increase your chances of success compared to secondhand materials. Consider making on-camera interviews with those who benefited most from your organization and including those in any multimedia presentation. This will also drive home the personal aspect of your pitch.

3. **That all donors want to meet with organizational leadership.** This is very untrue, Diriker says; some will be happy to conduct all their business just through you, the development contact. Simply making a standing offer to a major gift donor that he or she will always be able to get face-to-face time with your organization's higher-ups will often be reassurance enough.

4. **That donors give to desperate causes.** "No, they give to excellence and to proven organizations," says Diriker. In fact, desperation is often a huge turn-off during a major-gift pitch.

5. **That major gift donors will be happy to earmark their contribution toward whatever aspect of the organization that the organization itself deems a priority.** "No, they want to give to what they believe in," Diriker says.

*Source: Veronique Diriker, Director of Development, University of Maryland Eastern Shore, Princess Anne, MD.*
*Phone (410) 651-8142. E-mail: Vdiriker@umes.edu.*
*Website: www.umes.edu*

## Put Firm Numbers on Major Gift Solicitation

Outstanding fundraising comes not from guesswork but from hard data that goes back to the earliest stages of the solicitation process, says Christina Pulawski, principal of Christina Pulawski Consulting (Chicago, IL).

Pulawski says systematic and reliable fundraising includes understanding and calculating your organization's prospect yield — the percentage of solicited prospects who donate at the level you suggest.

Imagine you have 20 promising prospects identified, she says. Of these, you might be successful in approaching only 16 of them. Of these 16, you may qualify only 12 as having sufficient capacity and interest in your cause. Of the 12, you may succeed in actively cultivating only eight. Of the eight, cultivation might proceed far enough to solicit only four of them. And of those four, only one might say yes to the amount you request. Your average yield, then, is one out of 20, or 5 percent.

Overall, making these calculations will aid in understanding where your processes may be able to be improved, or where more or better information may be needed, says Pulawski.

Yield is a valuable metric in itself, but it can also be used to enhance major gift forecasting. Multiplying the total number of proposals planned over a certain period of time by the rate prospects are actually solicited by your organization, the solicitation yield and the average dollar amount of major gifts gives a reliable estimate of the revenue you can realistically expect to generate:

*(planned proposals) x (solicitation rate) x (yield)*
*x (average gift) = (total projected commitments)*

Pulawski says it's important to remember that at least six months to a year's worth of accurate data are often needed to generate remotely reliable projections.

*Source: Christina Pulawski, Principal, Christina Pulawski Consulting, Chicago, IL. Phone (773) 255-3873.*
*E-mail: c-pulawski@comcast.net*

## Business Advisory Committee Helps Broaden Support

If you believe your organization could be doing more to generate major gifts from businesses and the corporate community, establishing a business advisory committee is a wise use of time and resources.

Answers to these questions will provide insight into how such a committee might function and succeed in generating increased gift revenue.

### *Who should be on the business advisory committee, and how often should they meet?*

Begin with a smaller core group and expand over time. Enlist a handful of business community representatives who are already close to your organization as demonstrated through their past generous support. Be sure to include at least one board representative who can serve as a liaison to the full board.

To make the group's work meaningful, have them meet quarterly, if not monthly.

### *What should be their primary responsibilities?*

Members of this important group should be responsible for identifying, researching, rating and screening, cultivating, soliciting and stewarding major gift prospects within the business community. Obviously, the most important function of this committee is that of successfully soliciting gifts. Be sure to develop a committee job description to be shared with potential committee members before enlisting them. It's important that they know what's expected of them prior to joining your effort.

### *What can the development department do to help the business advisory committee succeed?*

Help guide their regular meeting procedures by developing a standard agenda they can follow each time. The agenda should include: reviewing and discussing prospects, making and accepting call assignments, reporting back on previous calls made and reviewing staff updates. Also, always incorporate some level of training and education that will help members be better prepared to fulfill their duties.

Once meetings have concluded, provide the follow-up support necessary to be sure committee members are completing their assignments. That may mean follow-up memos that confirm assignments and deadlines, one-on-one meetings to determine the status of calls and to address any questions or concerns and, at times, actually accompanying committee members on calls.

As your core advisory committee members become more adept at their jobs, you and they can explore expanding the group's numbers and expanding responsibilities.

## Turn Current Donors Into Estate Donors and Vice Versa

Frank Robertson, director of planned giving at the University of Minnesota Foundation (Minneapolis, MN), says that when it comes to fundraising, "we don't look at individuals as being either only estate donors or only current donors. Ideally, we think they should be both, and we think that, given the right circumstances, many will be."

Accordingly, Robertson and his staff encourage multiple forms of giving. One technique they use is what is known as the double ask. "The idea is that whenever you are asking for a major gift or an annual gift, you also bring up the idea of including the university in your estate plans," he says. "It's a relatively low-pressure approach and many of our development officers have come to really believe in it."

A robust stewardship process is another key to multiplying support, he says. All donors of future gifts, regardless of whether the amount is disclosed, receive membership in the university's Heritage Society. This introduces them to the stewardship process, which is important, according to Robertson.

"If someone is planning on establishing a scholarship upon their death, might they not want to start realizing that good work during their lifetime?" he says. "We find that including estate donors in the stewardship process not only cements their relationship with us and estate plans, but often leads to other outright gifts."

*Source: Frank Robertson, Director of Planned Giving, University of Minnesota Foundation, McNamara Alumni Center, Minneapolis, MN. Phone (612) 625-0893. E-mail: Rober038@umn.edu*

## Three Practical Strategies for Promoting Bequests

Since bequests are the most popular form of planned giving, it makes sense to continually promote them to your constituency. Here are three varied strategies for keeping the topic of bequests before your public:

1. **During any type of public gathering, never miss an opportunity to invite those present to consider your charity in their estate plans.** Whether your invitation is subtle or direct, mentioning the topic says it's important to your organization's future. If appropriate, state, "If you have made provisions but not informed us, please do."

2. **Don't be shy about publicizing the realization of a bequest.** The more examples the public sees, the more they realize your organization must be worthy of such gifts. These examples also provide you with additional opportunities to broadcast key messages: "Our board of trustees has approved a policy whereby all undesignated bequests will be directed to our endowment, thus perpetuating the donor's generosity for generations to come."

3. **Identify persons who share their intentions to include your charity in their estate plans and are willing to assist in encouraging others to do the same.** Determine ways such persons can help you promote bequests — testimonials at public functions, profiles in your newsletter or magazine, accompanying you on planned gift visits — and make use of their example. Engaging such willing individuals in your planned gift program will make them feel even more committed to your cause.

## Identify and Prioritize All Endowment Gift Opportunities

Whether you have a substantial endowment in place or you're just getting started in establishing one, it's important to take time to identify fundable endowment opportunities and prioritize their importance to your organization.

As much as you may be in need of unrestricted endowment gifts, the annual interest from which will underwrite yearly general operations, many donors prefer to earmark their investments to projects that can make a noticeable and visible difference.

As you gear up to market restricted endowment opportunities, follow this process:

1. Establish endowment parameters. At what level, for instance, can a donor have the choice of establishing a named fund? What's the maximum number of years donors will have to pay out endowment pledges? To what degree will you allow donors to spell out endowment restrictions?

2. Identify all endowment possibilities. List any existing restricted endowment accounts first. Then, review your organization's budget, first by category, then by line item. What categories and line items in your existing budget could be endowed?

3. Prioritize each identified endowment possibility based on two factors: 1) its importance to fulfilling your organization's needs and mission, 2) its "fundability" — its attractiveness to potential donors. After going through this process, you may decide that some potential endowment projects should be deleted or tabled. As you go through the final step, consider inviting small groups or individual potential donors to review your draft list and offer their opinions. The act of engaging them in the process at this point will help them to buy into investing in endowment. Plus, their responses will provide clues as to their funding interests.

Your final list of restricted endowment opportunities can be incorporated into marketing materials. In doing so, however, be sure that unrestricted endowment gifts top your invitation to invest.

*Sample restricted endowment opportunities:*

### RESTRICTED ENDOWMENT OPPORTUNITIES
### ABC ART CENTER

| ENDOWMENT OPPORTUNITY | GIFT MINIMUMS |
|---|---|

**Executive Director Fund** — Gifts directed to this fund will underwrite the salary and benefits of the executive director position, allowing us to attract the most capable individual the nation has to offer.....**$1 million**

**Lecture Series** — Fund will be used to underwrite an annual lecture series devoted to various aspects of arts topics. .............................**$250,000**

**Acquisition Fund** — annual interest purchases works for our permanent collection........................................................................**$100,000**

**Youth Education/Programs Fund** — Annual interest from this fund allows art center staff to ensure the future of arts programs and education relating to our region's youth. The size of the fund will determine the scope of new and expanded offerings...................................**$100,000**

**Annual Juried Artists' Exhibition** — This fund will underwrite our annual juried artists' exhibition and allow us to expand it further........**$50,000**

**Exhibit Fund** — Yearly proceeds underwrite cost of bringing exhibits to our facility.................................................................................**$50,000**

**Gift Shop Fund** — Yearly income will underwrite costs associated with the gift shop and allow us to enhance marketing efforts and retail opportunities for area artists' works....................................................................**$50,000**

## Five Steps to Building a Successful Endowment

Unrestricted endowments are one of the most dependable means of ensuring the long-term health of an organization. Nevertheless, they remain an untapped resource in many organizations.

Here James Connell, principle of the charitable estate and gift planning consultancy James E. Connell and Associates (Pinehurst, NC), explains the five keys to building a solid endowment:

1. **Establish policies and protocols.** Board-developed and approved policies should declare the purpose of the fund, whether it is restricted or unrestricted, what individuals or bodies will oversee it, what its minimum donation levels are, and what its spending formula will be. The minimum Connell suggests for an endowed fund is $25,000.

2. **Raise money for the endowment.** Applying all unrestricted bequests (or at least a sizable portion thereof) to the endowment is a powerful funding strategy, says Connell. "Boards might struggle with this, but using 'found money' like unrestricted bequests to pay for recurring expenses is bad long-term policy. Organizations need to be proactively planning for the future." To further fund a fledgling endowment, Connell suggests pairing endowment needs with annual fund and/or capital campaign solicitation efforts (see box at right).

3. **Invest endowment funds for long-term growth.** Boards' primary investment duties fall into two categories: asset allocation and analysis of performance. Regarding the first, Connell says most boards set up ranges of allocation. "They might say the equity portion will equal no less than 30 and no more than 60 percent of the overall portfolio. International asset exposure might be 10 to 25 percent; fixed income exposure might be 40 to 50." A fund manager can effectively handle funds of $1 million or more, he says, but smaller funds will often need to be managed internally by the board. This can best be handled through Exchange Traded Funds or low-cost comprehensive portfolios like Vanguard index funds.

4. **Determine a prudent spending formula.** A spending formula must determine both the amount that will be spent and the strategy for calculating portfolio distributions. In calculating the amount to spend, many organizations consider only the interest earned, but Connell cautions that spending must be based on the total return of the portfolio — both income and capital gains. As for performance, the evaluation standard will likely change over time. For the first three years, it will simply be the end of year value, he says. As the fund matures, sophisticated organizations will often switch to a three-year running average or a trailing 12-quarter average, both of which generate a smoother, long-term picture of performance, Connell says.

5. **Place year-end fundraising/corporate budget surpluses into the fund.** "Imagine your fundraising budget is $300,000 but you end up spending only $275,000. Since you were planning on spending that money anyway," he says, "the remaining $25,000 should be transferred to the endowment to provide for the future."

While endowments can be expanded almost indefinitely, Connell says a good initial target is a fund large enough to support the annual operations of the development program itself. If you have a $1 million budget and a payout rate of 4 percent, he says, you would need an endowment of at least $25 million. "That way you at least never have to worry about how you're going to fund the fundraising operation."

*Source: James Connell, Principle, James E. Connell and Associates, Pinehurst, NC. Phone (910) 295-6800. E-mail: Jec42644@aol.com. Website: www.connellandassoc.com*

### Incorporate Needs Into Annual/Capital Fundraising

To jump-start your new endowment, combine its fundraising efforts with those of annual or capital campaigns, says James Connell, principle of James E. Connell and Associates (Pinehurst, NC).

In a capital campaign, endowment needs can constitute a discreet goal unto themselves, says Connell. For example, you could set a $12 million goal for a $10 million construction project, with the surplus funding the endowment. Connell says this approach places the campaign in a context of long-term support and projects to the public a comprehensive message of foresight and ongoing development — a message that often gets lost in capital campaigns.

Annual fundraising can also support endowment objectives. Connell describes several ways to do so:

✓ The annual program goal could include an endowment goal as a subset of the appeal.

✓ When the annual fund goal is reached, all additional funds could be applied to the endowment.

✓ A set percentage of all annual fund gifts, e.g., 10 to 20 percent, could be allocated to the endowment.

✓ All annual gifts could be put toward a major endowment with wide donor appeal.

## Retained Life Estate Agreements Offer Many Advantages

Gifts of retained life estate — where a donor deeds property to a charity while retaining the right to use it during his/her lifetime — offer many advantages, particularly if a donor has no natural heirs or has numerous heirs scattered across the country, says Donna Roseman David, senior gift planning officer, Hartford Foundation for Public Giving (Hartford, CT).

Roseman David discusses elements that should be part of retained life estate agreements, based on the sample offered by the Hartford Foundation (right):

1. **Donor's right of usage.** Use of the property through the end of one's life is one primary benefit to the donor, says Roseman David. The right allows charities to receive larger gifts than the donor might otherwise be able to make.

2. **Donor responsibilities.** Properly structured agreements protect the charity from ongoing and upkeep expenses like taxes, utilities and assessments.

3. **Property damage.** This clause obliges the donor to assume repair costs or split insurance payments with the charity. Roseman David says donors usually provide certification of insurance and premium payment by adding the charity as an additional insured party on the policy, ensuring the organization receives copies of all relevant paperwork.

4. **Indemnity.** This clause provides further protection against cost and damages.

5. **Property inspection.** A gift of retained life estate is an asset, and organizations have a responsibility to protect their assets. Because every property and donor is different, she suggests using a professional inspection service prior to accepting the gift to determine the most appropriate type and frequency of inspection.

6. **Property modification.** This clause protects both the donor's right to improve the property and the charity's right to maintain the value of its asset.

7. **Amendment.** While a gift of remainder interest must be made irrevocably to provide the donor with tax advantages, an amendment clause offers both parties a way to refine arrangements regarding inspection, maintenance and such.

*Source: Donna Roseman David, Senior Gift Planning Officer, Hartford Foundation for Public Giving, Hartford, CT. Phone (860) 548-1888. E-mail: Ddavid@hfpg.org*

Content not available in this edition

# Fundraising Strategies for Small Shops

## WINNING SUPPORT THROUGH DIRECT MAIL SOLICITATION

*Direct mail appeals are an important part of well-rounded fundraising operations. Smaller nonprofits often find them particularly useful in expanding a limited base of donors and supporters. Direct mail campaigns require financial commitment, but when directed at receptive demographics, they can not only generate needed revenue, but build name recognition and mission awareness as well.*

## Map Out Yearly Direct Mail Appeals

To maximize gift revenue returns from direct mail, plan a year's worth of appeals in advance.

Using historical data, schedule a year's worth of appeals aimed at particular segments of your database (past contributors, nondonors, affinity groups, etc.), inviting support for particular funding projects.

There may be instances when an appeal is directed to your entire mailing list and others restricted to one or more segments of your database. Funding projects may vary from appeal to appeal as well.

Having a yearly schedule of appeals, such as the example shown here, helps to visualize the big picture and spot potential problems or missed opportunities. You may even choose to include other types of mailings (e.g.,

newsletters, invitations, announcements) in your schedule to visualize how various mailings play off one another.

### 2011 APPEALS SCHEDULE

| Date | Audience | Size | Project | Comments |
|------|----------|------|---------|----------|
| 1/15 | Past Contributors | 2,234 | Operations | |
| 3/1 | Past Contributors | 2,234 | Operations | Follow up: Non-responders |
| 4/15 | Area Businesses | 3,040 | Sponsorships | Multiple choices |
| 6/12 | Non-donors | 6,466 | Three projects | Multiple choices |
| 9/15 | Planned Gift Prospects | 883 | Planned gift invite | Includes bounce back |
| 11/15 | Lybunt Appeal | 2,234 | Operations | Follow up: Non-responders |
| 12/1 | Entire Database | 8,700 | Holiday Wish List | Multiple choices |

## Direct Mail Tips for Garnering Capable Donors

To add to your database of major gifts prospects, give this direct mail idea a test:

1. First, identify your city's or region's wealthiest ZIP codes. Next, approach a list broker to rent those ZIP codes for a one-time mailing. Compare your existing mailing list to the rented list and pull any duplicates.

2. Conduct a mailing to remaining names. Whether it's an introductory letter, series of letters or insider newsletters, include a bounce back with each that encourages recipients to ask for additional information about your organization and particular programs: special naming opportunities, endowment gifts, planned gifts and more.

While this direct mail approach probably won't result in immediate major gifts, it can be an important step towards introducing yourself and establishing an ongoing connection with financially capable individuals you may have previously missed.

## Put Direct Mail Pieces to the Test Before Sending

*Q. Why is it important to test print pieces before printing?*

"Without testing, you are missing out on one of the main advantages of direct mail marketing as compared to non-measurable forms of advertising and fundraising: response tracking means you don't have to guess at what works best. Testing is really the only way to ensure that you are reaching the right audience at the right time with the right message in the right format.

"Testing may appear to be costly, but in fact, the opposite is true. If you mail a newly created appeal to a list of prospective donors and it is not successful, you will not know why it failed and worse, significant monies may have been wasted. Was the list not appropriate? Was the package too expensive? Would there have been a better time to mail? There are a host of other questions without answers for any untested mailing. Testing provides benchmarks so that you can evaluate the success or failure of each effort. Improvements can be made in each effort to increase revenue over time.

"Testing also gives donors and prospective donors a voice in your decision-making process. Over time, their response to tests will let you know why, how and when they want to be approached for support, and how they prefer to participate in your programs."

*— Mary Richardson, Director of Strategic Planning, Huntsinger & Jeffer (Sarasota, FL)*

## WINNING SUPPORT THROUGH DIRECT MAIL SOLICITATION

### Eight Steps for Testing Direct Mail Pieces

What are the challenges of testing direct mail pieces for nonprofits? How can these challenges be overcome?

"The main challenge in testing is that it does represent risk," says Mary Richardson, director of strategic planning at Huntsinger & Jeffer (Sarasota, FL), a national full-service direct marketing agency specializing in nonprofit fundraising and commercial direct mail. "Testing is an investment in gaining knowledge — and that knowledge may or may not pay off in future returns."

To lessen the risk, nonprofits should test smart, Richardson says. Watch what competitors are doing, and keep a careful eye on your own results to identify potentially fruitful test opportunities. Allocate more of your budget to higher-potential variables such as audience and offer testing. Design and execute each test carefully and according to the rules of statistical probability. Repeat and confirm the promising tests before applying their results to your program.

The bottom line, Richardson says, is that while testing is somewhat risky, trying to run a direct marketing program without testing is far riskier.

Here, she shares eight tips for successfully testing direct-mail pieces:

1. **Decide what you need to know and how much you can budget to achieve your test objectives.** This is what you are willing to spend to gain knowledge — knowledge that can later be applied to the pursuit of net revenues.

2. **Identify the test variable.** Each test must be designed to evaluate only one variable, though you can include several tests in a campaign (e.g., Does use of first-class postage stamps on outgoing envelopes increase response and revenues, as compared with standard nonprofit stamps).

3. **Identify your audience.** For the postage test, let's say you want to measure the impact on donors who have contributed $50 or more within the past 12 months.

4. **Select records for your test cells.** You will need two test cells of equal quantity and quality. One will receive the mailing with nonprofit postage (This is the control panel.). The other will receive the mailing with first-class postage (This is the test panel.). Records should be randomly selected across your test audience (in this case, $50-plus current donors). In general, you will need panels of at least 5,000 records each for tests involving prospective donors or low-responding donor file segments, and should be safe with 2,500-name panels for tests involving current donors to ensure statistically reliable results.

5. **Develop and apply tracking codes** (usually personalized or printed on the reply forms) to distinguish between responses from each test panel.

6. **Mail both panels at the same time.**

7. **Analyze both costs and returns.** In this postage test, costs of using first-class stamps will be significantly higher than for the control nonprofit stamps. By analyzing both number of responses and revenues returned, you will learn if the additional cost is justified by an increase in response rate, average gift amount, net revenue, and/or the cost to raise a dollar.

8. **Repeat any test that looks promising,** confirming the results on a larger panel size whenever possible.

*Source: Mary Richardson, Director of Strategic Planning, Huntsinger & Jeffer, Sarasota, FL. Phone (941) 360-3339. E-mail: maryrich1@comcast.net*

---

### Testing Direct Mail? Watch for Red Flags

*Q. When testing direct-mail pieces, what red flags should you watch for?*

"Be sure you are comparing the costs accurately. Frequently, the control version in a test is being produced at a much larger quantity and its costs reflect volume-based production cost savings that are not available to the test panel. For the results analysis, equalize the comparison by getting and using cost quotations for the test panel as if it had been produced at the same quantity as the control version.

"Be sure to check that your results are statistically reliable. With a small number of responses, just a few can make a big difference in the response rate. Eliminate any 'extraordinary' gifts (often defined as $1,000 or more) that can throw off the revenue comparisons and are not likely to be repeatable. And remember that the results produced in each individual test are only a general indication of what you are likely to achieve in repeating the same test.

"That's why it's important to back-test, or repeat, a test to confirm the results before making any significant changes to your program."

— *Mary Richardson, Director of Strategic Planning, Huntsinger & Jeffer (Sarasota, FL)*

## WINNING SUPPORT THROUGH DIRECT MAIL SOLICITATION

## Use Timeline to Help Visualize Your Direct Mail Flow

How detailed is your direct mail production schedule for the fiscal year?

The use of a direct mail production schedule helps everyone in the advancement department see the big picture and anticipate what needs to be done when — and by whom — to keep all mailings on track. The production cycle of each direct mail piece — from writing to drop dates — can be more easily anticipated to ensure deadlines are being met. Such a schedule also helps planners visualize when various groups will receive direct mail to better plan broad-based cultivation procedures and anticipate the flow of incoming gift revenue.

If you're not already doing so, develop a direct mail production schedule similar to the example above to aid you in planning and visualizing your mailings for the entire year.

**2011 — DIRECT MAIL PRODUCTION SCHEDULE**

| Item and Audience | Responsible | Drop Date | June | July | Aug | Sept | Oct | Nov | Dec | Jan | Feb | March | April | May |
|---|---|---|---|---|---|---|---|---|---|---|---|---|---|---|
| Planned Gifts Newsletter | RKP | 7/15 | ▬ | ▬ | | | | | | | | | | |
| General Newsletter | DDS | 8/15 | ▬ | ▬ | ▬ | | | | | | | | | |
| Fall Appeal Letter #1 | MRT | 9/15 | | ▬ | ▬ | ▬ | | | | | | | | |
| Phonathon Postcard | GSC | 9/15 | | | ▬ | ▬ | | | | | | | | |
| Annual Report | JBS | 10/1 | ▬ | ▬ | ▬ | ▬ | | | | | | | | |
| Follow-up Appeal #1a | MRT | 10/20 | | | | | ▬ | ▬ | | | | | | |
| Invitations to $1,000+ Club Banquet | JBS | 10/20 | | | | | ▬ | | | | | | | |
| Planned Gifts Newsletter | RKP | 11/1 | | | | ▬ | ▬ | | | | | | | |
| Holiday Letter | MRT | 12/1 | | | | | | ▬ | ▬ | | | | | |
| General Newsletter | DDS | 1/15 | | | | | | ▬ | ▬ | ▬ | | | | |
| Planned Gifts Newsletter | RKP | 2/15 | | | | | | | ▬ | ▬ | | | | |
| Invitations to Special Event | MMG | 3/1 | | | | | | | | | ▬ | | | |
| General Newsletter | DDS | 3/15 | | | | | | | | ▬ | ▬ | ▬ | | |
| Spring Appeal Letter #2 | MRT | 4/1 | | | | | | | | | | ▬ | ▬ | |
| Invitations to $1,000+ Club Reception | JBS | 5/1 | | | | | | | | | | | ▬ | ▬ |

## Personalize Direct Mailings to Boost Audience Response

They all look the same — a No. 10 envelope with a computer-generated name label and photograph that plucks at your heartstrings. You don't need to open it to know it's an appeal for a gift.

When sending campaign mailings, realize that the little things mean a lot. Use personal touches such as these so the recipient knows someone was thinking specifically of him/her:

- Use a stamp instead of postal indicia.
- Hand-write an attention line to the recipient on the outside of the envelope.
- Place a self-stick note with brief hello on the brochure or in a blank space.
- Sign letters in a color different from the letter text to help distinguish it as an actual signature, not just a copy.
- Ask volunteers to write short notes to key donors to enclose in the mailing, such as "Dave, thanks for all your help," and sign their own names.
- Use brightly colored stamps or markers to draw the eye to key points.
- Refer in your letter to a specific instance or event the recipient knows about or attended. "It was gratifying to learn of your participation in our golf tournament," or "Your previous donations helped a great deal." Be sure the personalization fits a targeted, but sizable, group of individuals.
- Choose an unusual style of envelope and paper stock.
- Hand-address envelopes.
- Put names of both persons if mailing to a couple to instantly show them you recognize who they are.
- Mention in your letter a shared history with a large constituency, if possible, such as "Remember the thrill of winning the 1971 homecoming game and cheering for Paul Brown's last-minute touchdown?" Link this memory to your current topic. Choose an event many remember in a personal way.

## Completing the Direct Mail Package

Those materials that accompany your appeal letter — the pledge card, brochure, return envelope and so on — are also important to your overall package. How these pieces complement one another and convey messages all contribute to the effectiveness of the effort.

Here are pointers regarding the extras which make up your appeal package:

✓ Supporting materials in your package should reinforce your letter's message.

✓ Develop a reply or pledge card that stands on its own. Readers will be more likely to misplace or toss your letter than the reply card.

✓ Offer more than one payment option — credit card, monthly or quarterly payments.

✓ If you incorporate a photo, include a caption or identify the individual.

✓ Make your package easy to read by selecting a type font that is large enough and easily readable — factors important for senior citizens.

✓ Before your package is printed, have more than one individual proof each piece.

✓ Include your organization's phone and fax numbers on all printed materials. If online pledging is an option, list the website, and make sure it's up and running before your mailing is received.

✓ Have someone unfamiliar with your organization read the entire package to spot unanswered questions and identify inconsistencies.

✓ Your package design should promote your message, not confuse it.

✓ Clearly delineate each giving level and its associated benefits.

✓ Offer a special incentive for those who respond by a due date.

✓ Print "address correction requested" on all appeals to help increase contacts.

✓ Test the use of calendar giving envelopes with a portion of your constituency — one mailing includes 12 envelopes and encourages prospects to make monthly contributions.

✓ Put your package to the test: Ask someone to open your mailing and express their reactions as they go through it. Observe how they open it and consider if your piece could be put together more effectively.

✓ Keep paragraphs and sentences short to ensure ease of reading.

✓ Ask a respected colleague to read your completed letter (and accompanying materials) to review its impact, flow and grammar.

✓ If time permits, set your draft aside for a few days and then read it again.

## Nine Ways to Improve Direct Mail Appeals

With all of the competition for philanthropic dollars, appeal letters not only need to grab the attention of would-be donors, they need to be as compelling as possible, too.

By putting some thought into your letter and appeal package and paying attention to key details, you can increase both the number and size of gifts received from your mailings.

Here are nine ways to help give your 2009 appeal letters more of what it takes to move readers to make gifts:

1. Keep letters brief, neatly spaced, error free and grammatically correct.

2. Verify spelling of all names and proper titles of each individual.

3. Avoid use of words you wouldn't use in normal, everyday conversations. You don't want to look as if you studied your thesaurus just to impress them, and you don't want your readers to have to get out the dictionary to understand your message.

4. Use emotional adjectives sparingly. Almost every appeal leans heavily on "urgent" needs and "critical" situations. Convey your message with less-used but still-familiar, moving words.

5. Watch punctuation. Too many italicized, boldfaced or underlined passages clutter your page and detract from the message. Use exclamation marks only in proper context, not as an attention-getting gimmick.

6. Remember: Writing a short letter takes more effort than writing a long one. Ask an objective staff member to help with the editing process to make your piece as concise as possible while still having the impact you desire.

7. Don't send your first draft. Read your letter two or three times, or until all superfluous wording is eliminated.

8. Sign your name in real ink. Time taken to sign in a contrasting ink color shows you take a personal interest.

9. Be descriptive and direct. Writing "Volunteers spent more than 100 hours each weekend collecting canned goods," tells your story much better than cliches such as: "We are striving to set new standards of excellence in the services we offer to those in need."

## WINNING SUPPORT THROUGH DIRECT MAIL SOLICITATION

### Direct Mail Can Play Key Role in Securing Major Gifts

 *When it comes to major gifts, where might direct mail fit in? Does it play any role in helping your major gifts efforts?*

"We conducted a very successful direct mail campaign where we approached people who had never given before with a matching challenge tied into our 25th anniversary. The responses were very generous for direct mail, and the uniqueness of the campaign resulted in some news coverage, which also yielded new donor support."

— *Matthew M. Hoidal, Executive Director, Camp Sunshine (Casco, ME)*

"A nonprofit should tailor its direct mailers with a message that speaks to the desires of big donors, by writing specific copy that provides the benefits (that can only result from major gifts), denotes urgency and contains useful information — along with a call to action that's again specific to big donors. To get the best results, test different mailings beforehand to see what works best."

— *Melanie Rembrandt, CEO, Rembrandt Communications (Redondo Beach, CA)*

"Major gift officers can use a direct mail campaign to discover longevity donors who may emerge as major or planned gift prospects. When we notice that a donor has been giving for at least 10 consecutive years, we recognize that donor as a member of our Seller's Society. We then send a special letter from our Foundation president, thanking them for their longtime and consistent giving (no matter what the amount) and inviting them to come in for a hospital tour. In one case, this resulted in a donor calling and inquiring about any naming opportunities that might be available. Soon after, she contributed a $100,000 gift."

— *Niki Shafer, Vice President of Annual Giving, Nationwide Children's Hospital (Columbus, OH)*

### Analyze Appeal to Improve Future Results

Which of your direct mail appeals was most productive last year? Which resulted in the greatest dollar return? What was the average gift size from each mailing? How much did it cost to raise each dollar?

It makes good sense to monitor and analyze your direct mail costs and results throughout the course of each year and prior to drafting an operational plan for the upcoming year. Doing so will provide a quantitative measure of what works and what doesn't work.

Complete a direct mail cost analysis report (example shown below) to track costs and results of solicitation appeals throughout the year.

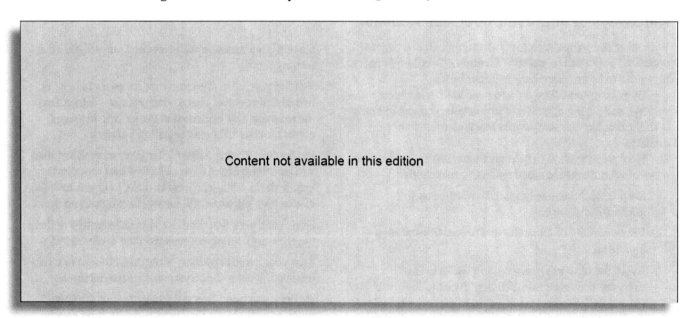

Content not available in this edition

*Fundraising Strategies for Small Shops.*
Edited by Scott C. Stevenson.
© 2011 Stevenson, Inc. Published 2011 by Stevenson, Inc.

# Fundraising Strategies for Small Shops

## CONTACTING DONORS AND PROSPECTS BY PHONE

*If in-person solicitation and direct mail represent opposing ends of the fundraising spectrum, telesolicitation falls somewhere in the middle — an approach that is neither too expensive nor too impersonal. Phone solicitation can be done one-on-one, but many organizations also rely on dozens of callers in periodic phonathon campaigns. To maximize the impact of such front-line callers, both paid and volunteer, employ the tips and suggestions found in the following articles.*

## Telesolicitation Can Increase Donor Participation Rate

Looking for ways to increase the donor participation rate among your constituency? Telemarketing strategies can certainly help boost your numbers.

Here's how to increase your donor participation rate by phone:

- Secure a challenge gift and inform nondonors that all new gifts to the annual effort will be matched dollar for dollar.
- Send a postcard menu of (affordable) gift opportunities two weeks prior to your phoning blitz.
- Divide your nondonor population into specific groups and target them by phone to support specific projects.
- Offer a special gift or incentive to those who make first-time gifts — calendar, cookbook, etc.
- Make an effort to match callers to nondonors they know.

- Compare your nonprofit's existing participation rate with similar organizations that have higher rates — establish a competitive spirit to surpass them.
- Rather than letting those called get by with "maybe," ask them to commit to a specific amount.
- Explain that your organization's chances for receiving foundation support will improve if you can demonstrate that a high percentage of your constituency contributes to your efforts financially.
- Ask nondonors for a gift in honor or in memory of someone they know and respect — former professor, retired agency employee or volunteer.
- Conduct a constituency survey among nondonors and ask them for a gift during the same call.

## Test Cold Calling as a Way to Acquire New Donors

Whether you'd like to bring in year-end dollars to boost your 2009 bottom line or start 2010 ahead of the game, one tried-and-true technique to consider is the cold call.

Calling current and former donors through annual phonathons is one reliable way nonprofits can renew gifts from these proven supporters. So why not test a targeted cold-call phoning effort exclusively aimed at nondonors?

Whether you use paid callers or volunteers, one caller or a dozen, conduct the effort over a two-week period or use a longer-term approach, be sure to create a script aimed at generating first-time gifts from those who have never given before.

To achieve success:

1. **Select three funding projects from which donors can choose** rather than asking for general support.
2. **Start small.** Ask for a modest gift — $15 or $25 — just to get these new individuals on board. Many people refuse to give just because they feel their modest contributions won't be appreciated or make any noticeable difference.
3. **Make it easy to give.** Offer credit card or installment payments — limit the number of payments for smaller gifts — and one-time cash payments.
4. **Offer special incentives.** Consider offering two or three inexpensive premiums for giving: free

admission to an event, one-year membership in one of your clubs at a reduced rate or a calendar with photos that relates to your organization and its mission.

Your goal should be simply to acquire new donors regardless of gift size. Once that's accomplished you can focus on building a habit of giving.

---

**Sample Phonathon Script Used for Nondonors**

**Caller:**

Mr. Hansen, this is Marci Wiggins calling on behalf of the Acme Gospel Mission. We're making a special effort this year to contact every citizen in our community to invite support for one of three special funding projects — and we're not asking for much.

Specifically, we would like you to consider a $15 or $25 gift to support one of these important projects:

1. New bedding for those who need shelter at our facility.
2. Meals for those we serve. A gift of $15 will cover meal costs for one needy person for one day.
3. Counseling services gifts to help get our visitors back on track.

Mr. Hansen, if you could find it in your heart to make a $15 or $25 gift for any one of these projects, you will receive two donated tickets for the Feb. 15 circus performance at Acme Auditorium. Which of these worthwhile projects would you like to fund today?

---

## How to Build and Grow a $500,000 Phonathon Fundraiser

How did the Mercer Island Schools Foundation (Mercer Island, WA) raise more than $480,000 in a phonathon lasting only two days and a total of about four hours?

Simple, says Penny Yantis, executive director of the foundation: experience. The school has been raising funds through the annual phonathon for 28 years.

Here's how it works: The phonathon is conducted over two weekday evenings in early autumn, but the campaign actually begins a month earlier when members of the foundation's board of directors call everyone who has donated $500 or more in the past year. These preparatory calls produce about half the total revenue while establishing leadership that is highlighted in all promotion of the general campaign.

The actual nights of calling are busy but organized. Around 160 volunteers gather at a central location (previously a local business, now several administrative buildings of the school district) and are first treated to dinner. They are then given a packet containing a name tag, sample script, instructions on how to organize their work space and a packet of 20 contact cards featuring an individual's name, phone number and other pertinent information such as the school a child attends, an alma mater or year of graduation.

Foundation officials give a 10-minute Microsoft Powerpoint presentation explaining packet contents, then volunteers begin making calls, working from about 6:45 to 8:45 p.m. In that time volunteers are generally able to complete about two packs of cards (40 contacts), with some 4,000 parents, alumni parents and grandparents, and selected members of the greater community being contacted over the duration of the two nights.

While many outgoing calls are not initially answered, the foundation plans for this. When contacts cannot be reached by phone, volunteers leave a voice message and follow up with a sorry-we-missed-you pledge envelope. Phonathon organizers sent some 700 such envelopes during the last event, and Yantis estimates that about a third were returned, increasing the two-night revenue by an additional 30 percent.

As volunteers complete calls, they affix mailing labels to pledge cards and place them in color-coded piles on their desk — green for affirmative pledges, orange for credit card pledges, yellow for problems like disconnected numbers, and red for "not this year" responses. Using these cards (instead of spreadsheet printouts) is critical to the event's functioning, says Yantis.

Because runners can collect and process the cards throughout the night, hundreds of pledge envelopes are ready for the mail just minutes after the event ends, instead of weeks.

Yantis also cites the volunteers making calls as a key to the fundraiser's success. Parents and teachers participate, but district administrators, principals and even city council members do as well. "Calls from a child's principal or the district superintendent are particularly effective," says Yantis with a laugh.

Yantis recommends phonathons to any nonprofit, noting they are particularly effective in smaller school districts. (Mercer Island has six schools and 4,000 students.) Hosting a phonathon for a group of this size ensures a more manageable number of calls and allows personal relationships to be more effectively leveraged. "Over the years we have been able to develop a culture where, when the school foundation calls, you just say yes," she says. "That's a real blessing."

*Source: Penny Yantis, Executive Director, Mercer Island Schools Foundation, Mercer Island, WA. Phone (206) 275-2550. E-mail: payantis@hotmail.com*

### Anatomy of a Phonathon

Part of the success of the phonathon hosted by the Mercer Island Schools Foundation (Mercer Island, WA) comes from the exhaustive logistical organization and step-by-step planning they do.

The volunteer call process instructions provide a great example and an excellent starting point for any organization looking to establish a similar fundraiser.

Let's take a closer look.

❑ **Step 1. Getting organized** — Volunteers are first given an inventory of the materials they should have received and encouraged to become familiar with them.

❑ **Step 2. Making the calls** — Next come instructions on how to handle call-making eventualities such as call blocking, answering machines and unreachable contacts. When volunteers do reach live contacts, they have a call script that walks them through several possible responses and conversation paths.

❑ **Step 3. Recording the call** — Following a completed call, volunteers learn where and how to record key information such as the contact's pledge response, amount of pledge, payment method and other supplementary notes.

❑ **Step 4. Preparing the pledge envelope** — Volunteers are given a photo of the pledge envelope that includes step-by-step instructions on how to prepare it, thus eliminating any confusion or mistakes.

❑ **Step 5. Preparing materials for pick up** — Finally, volunteers are shown how to sort and code their pledges to ensure the smoothest possible administrative processing.

## Second-ask Phonathon Raises More Than $18K for College

Development staff at Agnes Scott College (Decatur, GA) were in an enviable position with their alumnae challenge: They had secured enough donations to use all but $10,000 of matching funds available, up to $150,000. With some time left in the challenge, they decided to use the remaining funds as part of a phonathon to encourage prior donors to make a donation, offering the incentive of doubling the gift.

When the challenge money ran out one day before the phonathon, organizers chose to go ahead anyway and do a second ask to donors who had made gifts between July and December 2009.

The result? They raised more than $18,000 in one night. They also secured 60 pledges and a record 34 credit card gifts in one night of calling.

Joanne Davis, director of the annual fund, says, "Callers were told to thank donors, tell them the college had a very ambitious annual fund goal and ask if they could help us reach it by making a second gift."

Through the experience, Davis says, she and her staff learned that while the reason for the alumnae challenge was to encourage lapsed donors and alumnae who had never given to do so, the majority of those participating in the challenge were those who had already made a gift.

Davis says they were disappointed to have missed reaching their target audience, but were pleased to find out alumnae who had already given were excited by the challenge and willing to give again.

*Source: Joanne Davis, Director of the Annual Fund, Agnes Scott College, Decatur, GA. Phone (404) 471-5343.*
*E-mail: jadavis@agnesscott.edu*

## Five Tips for Building a Strong Phonathon Caller Base

The most important component for a successful phonathon is a solid and strong calling team, says Alicia Barnes, director of annual fund at Saint Vincent College (Latrobe, PA).

"We have a motto at our phonathon — it is not just a job. We are a 'phonathon family,'" Barnes says. "I do my best to make each student feel important and acknowledge how important the work they do is to the college and to future generations."

She cites five specific ways she works to build a strong phonathon caller base:

1. **Offering extensive training.** The college partners with IDC Fundraising Division, Harris Connect, LLC (Henderson, NV) to have a consultant conduct advanced-caller training for returning callers and new-caller training for all new hires.

2. **Individualizing incentive programs.** Each student is awarded a prize for each level hit in personal pledges ($1,000; $2,500; $5,000; and so on).

3. **Using an ask-back letter.** In these letters, Barnes provides key areas each caller needs to work on and thanks them for all their hard work.

4. **Offering special perks and team-building activities.** Barnes says one perk of being a returning caller is being able to move back to campus the Thursday before school starts for the fall semester. On Friday, callers have an all-day advanced-caller training. They receive a statistical analysis of the previous year's results. After the training is completed, callers participate in a group outing.

5. **Celebrating successes.** Barnes has an end-of-the-year celebration where she acknowledges all of the seniors, and passes out awards (e.g., Caller of the Year, Perfect Attendance, Credit Card Award, etc.).

Barnes says strategies like the ones detailed to the right can really take a phonathon program to the next level. "It makes the students feel valued, special, and in turn they truly take pride in their work and continually strive to do better."

*Source: Alicia M. Barnes, Director of Annual Fund, Saint Vincent College, Latrobe, PA.*
*Phone (724) 805-2499.*
*E-mail: alicia.barnes@ email.stvincent.edu*

### Telemarketing Tips

1. Have rookie callers seated next to productive veterans. They can listen and learn.

2. Handle rejection by thanking the contact and asking for his/her opinion about a matter affecting your organization. This helps the conversation conclude on a positive note.

3. If you reach an answering machine, try one of these methods: Mention a day and time you will call back; hold all answering machine calls until the weekend since most people tend to take calls then; or leave a message.

4. In addition to an overall phonathon goal, establish daily or nightly goals for your callers. Keep posting how much has been raised so far next to the daily goal.

## Equip Volunteer Callers With Solicitation Summary Reports

What documentation do you provide volunteers to help them make effective calls on your charity's behalf?

Volunteers and board members can be instrumental in soliciting gifts of all kinds — annual, major gifts, planned gifts and more. Their effectiveness, however, is a measure of how well-equipped they are before, during and after a call is made.

The solicitation summary report shown here serves as a valuable tool for volunteer solicitors. The one-page tool is intended to:

1. Provide a concise summary of the prospect along with his/her recent giving history.

2. Give specific instructions regarding type of call to be made.

3. Encourage the caller to record when the call was made, what took place and what follow-up steps should occur.

Although volunteers and board members involved in the solicitation process should receive appropriate training prior to making calls, the solicitation summary report becomes an important tool both prior to and following the call. Prospect profile information and instructions are valuable to the volunteer, and comments and follow-up advice are useful to staff and future volunteers involved with a particular call.

The following information is intended to help you better instruct volunteers as to the form's use:

1. **Prospect profile** — basic information intended to help the volunteer understand the individual's relationship with the charity and establish rapport with him/her.

2. **Objective** — provides a clear statement of expectation for the volunteer.

3. **Call outcome** — volunteer summarizes the call: To what degree the stated objective was met, along with any comments that may provide insight into the prospect's decision.

---

**SOLICITATION SUMMARY REPORT**

Prospect Name _____ Title _____
Organization _____
Address _____
Phone (W) _____ (H) _____

Relationship to [Name of Charity] _____
_____

Solicitation Target _____
Recent Giving History _____
Objective of Call _____
Name of Solicitor _____

Date of Call _____ Duration of Call _____

Met with Prospect at:
☐ Office    ☐ Residence    ☐ Other _____

Summary of Call's Outcome _____
_____
_____
_____

Recommended Follow-up _____
_____
_____
_____

_____    _____
SIGNATURE OF SOLICITOR              DATE

*Use this template to create an agency-specific solicitation summary report to help volunteers make effective calls on your organization's behalf.*

4. **Follow-up** — describes what future steps should be carried out (and when), based on the call's outcome.

5. **Volunteer's signature and date** report is turned in to the charity's office.

# Fundraising Strategies for Small Shops

## CREATING PROFITABLE EVENTS AND SIZABLE SPONSORSHIPS

*It is not uncommon for small organizations to generate a significant portion of their annual income from one or two large fundraising events. For such organizations, paying attention to a few key areas — budgeting, branding, promotion, etc. — can significantly increase event profitability and yearly revenue. Being more systematic and effective in securing corporate sponsorships can also have a huge impact.*

## Create First-time Event Budget

With so many factors to consider — from food to entertainment to decorations — how do you build a budget for a first-time event?

"The key is understanding costs for individual segments of the budget," says Cathy Genetti, president and founder of Next Level Event Design (Chicago, IL). "You need to know what to expect and what to budget for." Also, she says, have a "not-to-exceed" budget number early in the planning process.

Genetti shares steps she takes to help a nonprofit client determine a budget for a first-time fundraiser:

1. **Get a clear understanding of the organization's demographic**, events it has offered, the outcome of those events, and if they met expectations.

2. **Know the event goal.** The primary goal shouldn't be to raise money, but could be to create a closer community or increase awareness. Is there a call to action for the guests? What should be the emotional take-away?

3. **Articulate expectations and a shared definition of success.** Be realistic when planning an inaugural event and creating a count goal.

4. **Research other events** that may impact attendance.

5. **Determine how much money the event is expected to raise,** then do the math. Are sponsors or sponsorship opportunities involved? What is an appropriate ticket price for this demographic? Will ticket price merely cover the cost of the per-person price? How will additional sums be raised?

6. **Estimate the hours needed to produce the event,** including meetings, conference calls, walk-throughs and production time. Overestimate to accommodate unknown issues.

7. **Check with stakeholders** to make sure the initial rough figure will work for them.

"Normally there's one aspect of an event that is a main focus — it could be entertainment, food, lighting and décor, etc.," Genetti says. "Once you know this, you can earmark how much money you can allot to each category, so you can give this information to your vendors."

*Source: Cathy Genetti, President and Founder, Next Level Event Design, Chicago, IL. Phone (312) 280-1366.*
*E-mail: www.NextLevelEventDesign.com*

## Grab the Media's Attention

Looking to gain media attention for your event? You may want coverage in your local newspaper, but wonder where to begin.

Rebecca Leaman, a blogger with Wild Apricot (Toronto, Ontario, Canada), asked two acquaintances — one a longtime editor of a community newspaper and one a freelance reporter — how to make headlines.

Here, Leaman shares their insight into gaining media coverage for your event:

❑ **Get familiar with the publication.** Determine what kinds of stories the publication normally runs and if it typically uses press releases, photos with brief captions or human-interest features about local personalities.

❑ **Build a relationship with a reporter or editor.** Establishing a relationship with one or two reporters may win you a champion when it comes to pitching stories.

❑ **Get to the point of your pitch.** Don't call with a rambling intro to your organization, working toward asking for a story. Instead, ask how to submit an item to the local events calendar or other specific column.

❑ **Tell a good story.** Never mind the do-it-yourself public relations advice about reverse pyramid structure and press release formats; hook them with a story that practically writes itself.

❑ **Check the editorial calendar.** Does the paper have regular features or seasonal issues that fit with your schedule of activities, events and fundraising campaigns? If so, pitch them!

❑ **Put together a media kit.** Provide press releases, artwork photographs, logos, and other graphic elements, quotes from key individuals, contacts for more information and other assets that tell your story.

*Source: Rebecca Leaman, Wild Apricot Blogger and Jay Moonah, Wild Apricot/Bonasource Inc., Toronto, Ontario, Canada. Phone (416) 410-4059. E-mail: jay@wildapricot.com. Website: www.wildapricot.com*

## 10 Dos and Don'ts of Event Planning

Jodi Bos, principal of In Any Event by Jodi Bos, LLC (Grand Rapids, MI), has 16 years of experience as an event planner, including six years working in the nonprofit sector.

Here, Bos offers her most valuable dos and don'ts for event planning:

1. **Don't restrict your creativity because you have a limited budget.** There are so many ways to make an event look spectacular, even on a limited budget. For example, instead of using just one specialty linen in the room, mix three coordinating linens.

2. **Do consider signature drinks.** One hot trend in the event planning industry is offering signature drinks during cocktail hour. Adopt this trend at your next fundraiser. Not only is it creative, it's cost effective.

3. **Don't skimp when it comes to centerpieces.** Budget enough money for a substantial centerpiece. Pay attention to scale when creating a beautiful table. If you can't allocate additional funds to centerpieces, consider an alternative such as displaying the dessert in the center of the table.

4. **Do get crafty and embrace your local thrift store.** For a recent fundraiser produced on a limited budget, Bos scoured local thrift stores for brass candlesticks, acquiring more than 200. Bos and her staff cleaned and spray painted them with enamel paint, added white taper candles and clustered the candlesticks in groups on the tables, making the room glow in candlelight.

5. **Don't be afraid to mix table shapes and sizes when** designing your room layout. There's nothing more boring than a room full of round tables. Mix it up with a combination of round, square and rectangular tables.

6. **Do think outside the box when selecting the time of your event.** Breakfast and lunch events are incredibly cost-effective. You might be surprised to find that more people attend a fundraiser that is held in the morning than one held in the evening.

7. **Do browse event-planning magazines and websites.** Adapt ideas to your event.

8. **Don't be afraid of color and texture.** Create event décor using the principles of color and texture that you see in fashion. Gone are the days when an event is decorated in just red, for example. Now, you see red paired with aqua and accented with black.

9. **Do check Craigslist often.** You'll be amazed at what people sell there. You'll find brides selling all of their leftover wedding décor like apothecary jars, glass vases used for centerpieces and candles. You can snap these treasures up for pennies on the dollar, and put them to good use at your next event.

10. **Don't be afraid to try something unique when it comes to food.** Offer food stations where guests roam around a room and mingle while eating, or serve dinner family-style where guests pass serving dishes around the table.

*Source: Jodi Bos, Principal, In Any Event by Jodi Bos, LLC, Grand Rapids, MI. Phone (616) 541-0020. E-mail: info@in-any-event.org. Website: www.in-any-event.org*

## Create and Update Vendor Pricing Binder

Nonprofits that manage a multitude of events throughout the course of the year will benefit by creating a vendor pricing binder and keeping it up-to-date.

Follow these simple steps for creating a system of evaluating and monitoring vendor pricing:

❑ Create a binder that is complete with copies of your most recent vendor invoices from your key events.

❑ Send bid requests to three (or more) suppliers or vendors within each category — catering, venue, flowers, beverage supplier, decorator, etc. — that you most commonly contract. For example, if you tend to rent space for your large annual events, find three venues similar in size and capacity and request pricing from all three. Once these bids are collected, create a spreadsheet that offers you at-a-glance evaluation of pricing. Also, mark the date you received each bid and keep copies of each bid under a section headed by the individual vendor's name.

❑ Assign the task of updating this information every six months to a dedicated volunteer or intern. Ask this person to send bid requests to the same vendors every six months and update the binder accordingly. Retain previous bids to evaluate how costs have increased with each vendor.

❑ In addition to updating pricing, also update the contact names and information of the appropriate contact person(s) with each vendor site.

❑ Make it a goal to obtain bids from new vendors or venues that open in your region or established ones you've not worked with in the past. Doing so will open new doors, and possibly offer a wider variety of price points, when planning events.

The effort you put into creating this useful tool will pay off when preparing and planning your next event, giving you an effective resource to evaluate current price, service and any changes within the industry, and helping you maximize profit while minimizing planning time.

## Blueprint for a Half-million-dollar Fundraiser

The Spring For Schools Luncheon of the Bellevue Schools Foundation (Bellevue, WA) draws more than 1,000 guests and raises more than $500,000 each year. Marian McDermott, manager of institutional giving, shares elements central to the event's success:

✓ **Guests in the door**. "Our priority is getting guests in the door, so we don't sell tickets," McDermott says. Rather, a volunteer-run audience development committee recruits a body of table captains who, in turn, recruit the event's many attendees.

✓ **Corporate sponsorship.** In 2010, corporate sponsorship accounted for about a fifth ($117,000) of all funds raised at the luncheon. Bellevue benefits from major area corporations like Microsoft and Boeing, but McDermott says smaller businesses are major sponsors as well. "We actively recruit board members from the business community to stay as closely connected as we can," she says. "We are always making the case that good schools produce good employees and help attract good recruits from across the country and around the world."

✓ **Targeted giving campaigns.** The event's general fundraising efforts are bolstered by two targeted giving campaigns: The Angels matching campaign invites major donors to contribute $10,000 to a fund that matches gifts up to $1,000, while the Head of the Class campaign invites prominent community members — many of them high-profile business leaders — to pledge leadership gifts ($1,000-plus) in advance of the event. These gifts, recognized in the luncheon program, provide a powerful example for others to follow, says McDermott.

✓ **Coordinated ask.** Each year, the luncheon includes a suggested specific donation for guests. The most recent suggestion was $200 per guest. This amount is communicated to guests by the table captains, all of whom receive thorough training and preparation six weeks prior to the event (see illustration).

*Source: Marian McDermott, Manager of Institutional Giving, Bellevue Schools Foundation, Bellevue, WA. Phone (425) 456-4199. E-mail: Marian@bsfdn.org*

Content not available in this edition

*The success of the Spring For Schools Luncheon of the Bellevue Schools Foundation (Bellevue, WA) depends in large part on a small army of table captains. Foundation development staff carefully coach table captains to help them succeed using tools such as this handout.*

## CREATING PROFITABLE EVENTS AND SIZABLE SPONSORSHIPS

### Post-event Survey Engages Participants, Provides Ideas to Improve Future Events

A post-event survey can give you a deeper understanding of attendees' impressions and, more importantly, how to improve the event so that they'll return the next year and bring their friends.

"We've had times when feedback from participants has been polar opposites — what one person loves, another one doesn't like," says Dona Wininsky, communications director, American Lung Association (ALA) in Wisconsin (Brookfield, WI). "What we're mostly looking for is a meaningful way to connect people to our mission while offering them a fun way to support the organization and learn more about us."

The ALA chapter hosts a Fight for Air Climb in spring and a Fight for Air Walk in fall. Money raised at both events goes toward education, research and advocacy for lung disease.

"We want to not only be financially successful, but have (these events) be a fun and rewarding experience for the participants and help raise awareness of the work we do," Wininsky says.

ALA officials ask participants to fill out a 31-question post-event survey created using SurveyMonkey (www.surveymonkey.com).

Climb participants receive a link to the online survey in an end-of-event e-mail. Walk participants receive a hard-copy survey in the mail with a letter thanking them for their participation.

While the ALA uses post-event surveys for both events, officials say they have a better return rate among walk participants than climb participants.

Angie Glenn, special events manager, notes the walk is very family-oriented while the climb brings in people of all fitness levels who are climbing for the physical challenge of it. "The walk has more participants with direct tie-in to our mission and, while many climbers are tied to our mission, many are not," says Glenn, explaining the higher survey response from walk participants. "If they feel that personal connection, I think they are more likely to complete the survey."

*Sources: Dona Wininsky, Communications Director; Angie Glenn, Special Events Manager American Lung Association in Wisconsin, Brookfield, WI. Phone (262) 703-4200.*

Content not available in this edition

## CREATING PROFITABLE EVENTS AND SIZABLE SPONSORSHIPS

## Six Reasons to Have Sponsorship Guidelines in Place

Sponsorship guidelines are like New Year's resolutions. They sound like a good idea, but they require time, energy and commitment to put in place and follow. But that shouldn't prevent you from putting sponsorship guidelines in place, says Tim Griswold, executive director and founder, Foundation for Caregivers (Chantilly, VA).

"I come from the for-profit world (where I) saw published guidelines to be as logical as having published service policies for a business," Griswold says. When he moved into the non-profit world, he says, "I found the absence of guidelines to be quite surprising."

So Griswold and board member Mary Madsen started creating policies that would make them accountable for what they were saying and let prospective sponsors know what the Foundation for Caregivers stood for and represented.

The process has been educational, says Griswold, who shares six reasons why sponsorship guidelines are worth having:

1. They simplify communications. When communicating with prospective sponsors you point them to your guidelines.

2. Sponsorship guidelines keep you honest. It is easy to compromise your standards if you are the only one who knows those standards. When you post them for everyone to read, it makes it really difficult to take shortcuts.

3. Sponsorship guidelines convey professionalism. If your organization is just starting out, guidelines let people know you are serious.

4. Sponsorship guidelines force clarity. The process of writing the guidelines forces you to make sure you don't mislead or paint your way into a corner.

5. Sponsorship guidelines force you to work through the details. Setting guidelines will require you to address questions or issues you may have glossed over or left until a later date.

6. Sponsorship guidelines inform sponsors. Guidelines let them know you are aware of risks associated with sponsorship and what you are trying to do to mitigate those risks.

View the foundation's sponsorship guidelines at: www.ffcg.org/sponsorship.htm

*Source: Tim Griswold, Executive Director and Founder, Foundation for Caregivers, Caldwell, ID. Phone (208) 318-3144. E-mail: tgriswold@ffcg.org*

## Questions Help Develop Sponsorship Guidelines

Tim Griswold, executive director and founder, Foundation for Caregivers (Chantilly, VA), says sponsorship guidelines are a great way to clarify your organization's stance on fundraising partnerships. But what should you consider when you are creating sponsorship guidelines for your organization?

Asking yourself these questions will provide a step in the right direction:

❑ What are your organization's core beliefs?

❑ What should be covered? How detailed should you get?

❑ What are you seeking sponsorship for?

❑ What are your fundraising goals?

❑ Who would you like to partner with? Is there anyone you would not partner with? Why? How will you convey that?

❑ Do certain sponsors represent conflicts of interest or even the perception of a conflict of interest?

❑ Will you offer category exclusivity to certain types of businesses?

❑ Will sponsors have any say in program content or collateral materials?

❑ What benefits will sponsors receive? What responsibilities will they have?

❑ Are there any risks associated with sponsorship? If so, how are you minimizing the risks?

## CREATING PROFITABLE EVENTS AND SIZABLE SPONSORSHIPS

### Enhance Sponsorship Revenue

Sponsorships — or lack of them — can be the difference between a prospering event and a floundering one.

To augment this critical stream of revenue, Jean Block, president of Jean Block Consulting Inc. (Albuquerque, NM), advises event organizers to:

❑ **Seek mission-matched sponsors**. In seeking sponsors, look for businesses that have a natural affinity for your mission, the people you serve or the people who will attend your event. Less-traditional sponsors (e.g., businesses outside your immediate industry area) can be a significant source of untapped potential.

❑ **Own the value of your event**. Your event is an important opportunity for sponsors to connect with potential customers, so own that value, says Block. "Businesses are often looking for more impact and visibility. Do some brainstorming, make a list of who would benefit from access to your events and attendees, and approach them with the opportunity to participate."

❑ **Rethink sponsorship benefits**. Do sponsors really care about the banner in the back of the room or the information table in the hall? Ask long-time sponsors what benefits they would find most valuable.

❑ **Over-deliver on promises**. Numerous nonprofits seek corporate support, so differentiate yourself from the pack by delivering the benefits you promise — and then some, says Block.

❑ **Thank each sponsor at least three times**. The first gesture of appreciation should be a handwritten note as soon as a pledge is received. The second should warmly acknowledge the receipt of payment. The third should come after the event, and should enumerate the event's concrete results — dollars raised, programs funded, etc. — that the donor's support made possible.

*Source: Jean Block, President, Jean Block Consulting Inc., Albuquerque, NM. Phone (505) 899-1520. E-mail: jean@jblockinc.com. Website: www.jblockinc.com*

### Keep Sponsors Year to Year by Offering Right of First Refusal

As a sponsorship benefit, sponsors of the annual conference for the Association of Air Medical Services (Alexandria, VA) have right of first refusal on future conference sponsorships.

"Right of first refusal" means that the association will contact the sponsoring company prior to allowing someone else to pick up on the sponsorship for the coming year, says Blair Marie Beggan, communications and marketing manager.

"Once a company has sponsored any item or special event for one year," Beggan says, "they always have the option to renew the sponsorship for the following year before it is offered as an option to another company."

Offering the right of first refusal to current sponsors means those sponsors don't have to keep track of the sponsorships they want to support because they know that the association will contact them each year, says Beggan.

"Offering the right of first refusal helps to build long-term relationships between our organization and our corporate members," she says. "As a small nonprofit, we simply could not hold such a robust and quality conference without the partnerships with our corporate sponsors."

To remind sponsors of their right of first refusal, Beggan calls each sponsor to gauge interest level for the upcoming year.

About 90 percent of their sponsors take advantage of the right of first refusal benefit, she says: "Our niche industry is fairly close-knit. I have the luxury of one-on-one relationships with all of my sponsors. It is rare to have a sponsor drop out of the program. Even in the economic downturn over the past year, only two opted out of their sponsorship, and in one of those cases, I was able to work with them to find something that would be a better fit for their budget."

*Source: Blair Marie Beggan, Communications & Marketing Manager, Association of Air Medical Services, Alexandria, VA . Phone (703) 836-8732. E-mail: bbeggan@aams.org*

*Fundraising Strategies for Small Shops.*
Edited by Scott C. Stevenson.
© 2011 Stevenson, Inc. Published 2011 by Stevenson, Inc.

# Fundraising Strategies for Small Shops

## MESSAGING AND PUBLIC RELATIONS

*Effective fundraising hinges on an organization's ability to get its story out to the public. Large organizations have a public relations department to accomplish that, but smaller ones often rely partly or entirely on development staff. From blogs and social media outlets to mission statements and traditional mailers, mastering the tools of public communication will benefit all phases of your fundraising cycle.*

## Make Your CEO's Message Purposeful

Many annual reports published by charitable institutions contain a rarely read block of text on the inside cover or first page: a message from the president or chief executive officer. Most readers spot words like excellence and commitment, anticipate the rest and move on — especially when times are stable and there has been little bad news.

As a development officer, you may be asked to write such a message for your leader or to suggest content for a message he/she writes and asks you to edit.

Here are strategies you can consider:

*When you write the message —*

- **Know how your CEO thinks and speaks.** Some of the most eloquent speakers feel uncomfortable with written communications. Is the CEO plain spoken and informal or an amateur actor who has played Hamlet with good reviews? Written messages should be consistent with speaking and personal style.
- **Do an interview before writing.** Ask your CEO what issues should be addressed and what he/she wants to say to readers — in order of importance. Emphasize the primary objective of the message — to thank, to convey achievements, to invite support, etc.
- **Prepare a draft for review.** Write the message as you see fit, then offer it to your CEO for approval. Ask that all changes be made quickly and returned to you.

*When you are the editor —*

- **Your CEO may be an articulate writer.** Consider yourself lucky if his/her copy is clean and concise. But do offer a small list of suggestions that are of great current interest to your donors. In your position, you may be more attuned to issues or questions about which your constituency may wish to know.
- **Discuss the content of the rest of the publication.** If your annual report has a special theme and a common thread throughout each section, be sure the CEO is familiar enough with each so the message will complement other content.

- **If your CEO writes poorly but thinks he/she writes well, it is time to use your diplomatic skills.** The message may be long and cumbersome. Tell him/her you have read it, but space will be tight — ask if he/she can shorten it. The second phase includes your own subtle editing (without changing the meaning of any phrase) by eliminating unnecessary words. When you resubmit it, the subtle changes may very well go unnoticed, or the improvements may be appreciated.
- **Ask first if your editing is acceptable before the message is written.** Communication is a key when the CEO actually expects you to clean it up, but you don't for fear of causing ill will. Talk about editing preferences at the first opportunity — if you haven't seen his/her writing before, you aren't being judgmental, but courteous. You simply want to know what is expected of you as editor of this and other publications.
- **Collect several CEOs' messages from other organizations.** Have a sampling of both good and poor examples to build your case for brevity. Send each to the CEO as an FYI with your succinct summary of each stack: "These were brief but meaty," or "Notice how many words these writers used to say nothing?"
- **Offer a list of words to use or avoid.** One major problem with CEOs' messages is overuse of cliché words such as dedication, excellence, commitment and teamwork. Encourage your CEO to find as many fitting, simpler replacements as possible. Such simplification leaves a more heartfelt impression.

## Blogging for Bad Writers

Does your CEO swear he or she can't blog or worry that his or her words will sound too wooden? Get the creativity flowing with these tips:

- ✓ Go for casual. "I use slang, bad grammar, bad punctuation, sarcasm, and I break a lot of rules," says Diane Scimone, founder and director of Born To Fly International (Lake Mary, FL) and a former journalist.
- ✓ Don't be afraid to be funny. "I try to make my posts entertaining," says Antonia Namnath, founder and CEO of Weight Loss Surgery Foundation of America (Davis, CA).

- ✓ Keep it short! It's better to write five short posts than one long one, says Scimone. Chop a longer piece into a series of shorter posts, adding tune-in-tomorrow suspense.
- ✓ Stumped for a subject? Visit www.google.com/trends for the day's most-searched words or phrases.
- ✓ Just write. Write with feeling, says Scimone. "Tell a story, or tell your story.... If people want to read a news report, they'll go to CNN.com. They want stories about you and the cause you're passionate about."

## Why Have a Fundraising Mission Statement?

Most nonprofits have a mission statement that guides the entire organization, but the institutional advancement office at Xavier University of Louisiana (New Orleans, LA) also has its own mission statement.

"Having an institutional advancement mission statement helps guide us as a division as to what our role is," says Kenneth St. Charles, Ph.D., vice president of institutional advancement. "It helps me, as a leader, to ensure that we have a vision for working together. For donors, they can see the values that we as a division ascribe to."

Xavier's institutional advancement mission statement is posted on its website (www.xula.edu/institutional-advancement/index.php). "We keep it on our website so that we can keep it as fresh as possible," says St. Charles. "It's a living, breathing document."

The mission statement is reviewed as needed, he says, noting that they most recently reviewed it earlier this year as they prepared for an accreditation visit.

The institutional advancement mission statement is subordinate to the university's mission statement. "We wouldn't want our mission statement to receive more prominence than the university's mission statement," says St. Charles.

To create an institutional advancement mission statement, St. Charles advises:

✓ Make sure your institutional advancement mission statement reflects values stated in your organizational/institutional mission statement.

✓ Seek input from stakeholders who will have to live up to the values of the mission statement, including divisions outside of the institutional advancement office. One person cannot create it alone.

✓ Be flexible. It will take some time to accurately capture everyone's input.

✓ Look for models of mission statements from other organizations and universities that you can replicate.

✓ Talk to your colleagues at other organizations and universities and share drafts of your mission statement with them for feedback.

*Source: Kenneth St. Charles, Ph.D., Vice President Institutional Advancement, Xavier University of Louisiana, New Orleans, LA. Phone (504) 520-5797. E-mail: kstcharl@xula.edu*

## Make the Message Match the Audience

Staff at the Performing Arts Workshop (San Francisco, CA) rely on social networking options to communicate important information. Anne Trickey, program and communications coordinator, says she has worked to glean which groups in the organization's constituency respond best to particular types of messaging. She shares some of her findings, and how she uses that information to better match the message to its intended audience:

❑ **Facebook and other social media**: "In our July 2010 newsletter, we sent out a request for our entire database to become fans of (or Like) the Performing Arts Workshop on Facebook. We've found it's a good way to get immediate response; people can see pieces of information that give them a good feeling about what we do (and) immediately RSVP to events or comment on what we're doing. It may not be as beautiful to look at as an e-mail newsletter, but an e-mail takes more work to put together — it has to be structured and messaged as a whole. A Facebook post can be brief. Here, we reach a smaller donor base, (and) they are most likely to take action on the Internet."

❑ **Traditional mail and word of mouth:** "Older donors respond best to this type of communication — which, in our case, is most of our donor base. These donors are more likely to get behind a campaign than the people who are plugged in to the Internet, so it's important to speak to them where they will hear it. For them, we focus on results and communicate youth outcomes — success stories from within the community. We involve site partners, schools and communities to communicate how the children are learning '21st century skills, creative expression and self efficacy.' That's our message. It mobilizes people."

❑ **YouTube:** "People who have seen our videos on YouTube tend to be outside of what we think of as our constituency, which is to say we haven't solicited them. But here, we are expanding our pool of supporters, which strengthens the organization." One of the biggest struggles for a group like theirs, she adds, is finding artists who are also great teachers "who understand what we want them to do, and are good in the classroom. When we attract artists who are really engaged in what we do, that gets results. And results attract donors."

*Source: Anne Trickey, Program and Communications Coordinator, Performing Arts Workshop, San Francisco, CA. Phone (415) 673-2634 E-mail: anne@performingartsworkshop.org. Website: www.performingartsworkshop.org*

## Master Three Key Elements of Fundraising Communication Plan

A well-conceived communications plan is essential to the success of any major fundraising campaign, says Tony Poderis, an independent fundraising consultant and former director of development for the Cleveland Orchestra (Cleveland, OH).

Poderis cites three elements indispensable to any communications plan:

1. **A Persuasive Case for Support** — "A properly executed case for support is perhaps any organization's most powerful tool in persuading prospective donors," says Poderis, noting that it can also be used to recruit volunteers and additional solicitors. The points Poderis says a well-presented case for support should make include:

   - Let's break the ho-hum barrier (introduction designed to engage interest in organization and problem/challenge).
   - We're relevant within a broader context (if appropriate, a brief overview of how the problem we're addressing may reflect a more global problem).
   - We're proud of our past (history of organization).
   - Please read on (here's what is special about our organization; the value of our programs and services).
   - Here's a compelling challenge that deserves your attention (we have carefully assessed the need).
   - We did our homework before embarking on this campaign (thoroughness of initial planning and research).
   - We can make it work (We have the organization and resources to accomplish our objectives).
   - What's in it for you (here's your opportunity to do something heroic)?
   - Do it now, please! (We're asking you to take action now, and we will make it easy for you to do so.)

2. **A Winning Campaign Brochure** — Having an official brochure in hand is essential in establishing the perception in potential donors' minds that the campaign is professional and in providing confidence to solicitors, Poderis says. Include in campaign brochures:

   - Campaign chair's message.
   - Campaign chair and committee roster.
   - Mission and vision.

   - Overview of background and history.
   - Programs and services.
   - Case for support of particular project/ assessment of need.
   - Drawings, tables and diagrams relating to the campaign.
   - Ways to give (cash, stock, in-kind contributions, multi-year installments).
   - Roster of board of trustees, staff.
   - Named gift opportunities for endowment and capital campaigns.
   - Membership categories for annual fund campaigns.
   - Endorsements and support quotes from civic, corporate and government leaders, typically incorporated graphically throughout the brochure.
   - Acknowledgements for donated and in-kind services for campaign publications.

3. **A Definitive Schedule for Publicizing Your Campaign** — Publicity is a must for any major fundraising campaign, but Poderis says it should be sought not for its own sake but to support and enhance the fundraising effort. "Publicity in the case of a fundraising campaign is nothing more than the scheduling of announcements and events at intervals which will work to achieve your goal," he says, adding that these events should be committed to a timetable and incorporated into the campaign's overall calendar. Common milestones Poderis uses to gain publicity include:

   - Introduction of campaign chair, campaign goal, volunteer campaign leaders and solicitors.
   - Campaign kickoff event with planned civic and community leader participation.
   - Status of major gifts received, as appropriate, including significant named gift announcements in the case of capital and endowment campaigns.
   - Ground breaking, in the case of capital campaigns.
   - First major gift received.
   - 25, 50, 75 and 90 percent of goal reached.
   - Total goal reached.
   - Dedication, in the case of a capital campaign, and a celebration in the case of every campaign.

*Source: Tony Poderis, Independent Fundraising Consultant, Willoughby Hills, OH. Phone (440) 944-9230. E-mail: tony@raise-funds.com*

## Eight Tips for Writing Engaging Website Copy

Whether launching a new website or redesigning an existing one, keep some key tips in mind when developing the all-important copy that will fill your Web pages.

Joyce Remy, senior editor with the communications firm, IlluminAge Communication Partners (Seattle, WA), offers information that can help nonprofits create website content that both meets the needs of Web users while getting the most value from their website investment:

1. **Consider the other reader — the search engine.** For search engines to find website pages, the pages must include keywords likely to be used by people trying to find your organization. If your organization is a food bank, use terms on your site such as "feeding the hungry" and "food shelf." "As you craft copy, it is important that your keywords sound natural to the readers," says Remy.

2. **Web users are usually seeking a particular piece of information.** Unlike a brochure or ad, websites come with high expectations as an information source, Remy says. "Tailor your language accordingly, offering customers concrete facts, engagingly presented, about all the services your organization offers."

3. **Users navigate your site in a non-linear fashion.** Because Web users can move freely through the site, it is vital that your text doesn't depend on information found on previous pages. Make a good impression on every page, realizing that page users may arrive on a page other than your home page as they navigate the Web.

4. **Persons read Web pages differently than they read other types of copy.** Remy says studies indicate website visitors usually begin with a quick initial once-over when visiting a page. Visual cues such as short paragraphs, bullet points, subheads and white space ensure they can find what they want quickly.

5. **Compared to the printed page, reading on a computer screen is hard work.** As you begin constructing your text, write long and edit to short. Once your basic points are captured, you can usually trim quite a bit and not lose the meaning.

6. **The text of your website doesn't stand alone.** Elements such as logo and contact information, images, navigation buttons and consistent footers allow users to quickly figure out what is available on the site and constantly interact with your text. This can help keep copy concise.

7. **Hyperlinks add a new dimension.** This option allows readers to go to a different spot on the page, different page on your site or to another site entirely. "Hyperlinks give your users the choice of learning about something in greater depth, but don't overdo it," Remy says. "Links can be distracting, and once readers leave a page, they may not return."

8. **Use website content area wisely.** "Viewers may not know about your organization. Be clear, concise and thorough when describing the services, geographic areas served and your organization's history, staff or philosophy."

*Source: Joyce Remy, Senior Editor, IlluminAge Communication Partners, Seattle, WA. Phone (800) 448-5213. E-mail: joyce@illuminage.com*

*Fundraising Strategies for Small Shops.*
Edited by Scott C. Stevenson.
© 2011 Stevenson, Inc. Published 2011 by Stevenson, Inc.

# Fundraising Strategies for Small Shops

## BUILDING A FUNDRAISING BOARD

*Of all the challenges facing small nonprofits, perhaps none are as important as where to find prospects of significant financial capacity. Organizations across the country face this question and many of them come to the same conclusion: their board of directors. Board members can supply large portions of both annual and capital funding needs, and nurturing a financially capable board — both "givers" and "getters" — is, therefore, a great step toward long-term financial security.*

## Set Getting Expectations for Individual Board Members

Having difficulty convincing board members to raise annual support on behalf of your cause? Set clear expectations.

In addition to their own giving, you may want individual board members to assume responsibility for getting annual gifts from friends and associates. To encourage that, share ways in which they can make that happen. Offer examples of how they could meet individual getting goals, such as:

- Establishing a challenge gift for friends and associates, "I'll match whatever you give up to $X."

- Selling a minimum of X tickets to a fundraising event.

- Hosting a $X per person dinner at your home.

- Convincing a minimum of X businesses to write a check or provide a gift in kind of products or services.

Sometimes board members are willing to ask others for support; they simply want some options for how they can make that happen.

## Seven Ways to Boost Board Member Fundraising

The well-worn adage of "time, talent and treasure" is insufficient for the demands of modern fundraising, says Justin Tolan, chief fundraising adviser at the nonprofit consultancy ME&V (Cedar Falls, IA). "Donors are more savvy than ever, and board members absolutely have to lead by giving, at least to the degree that they are capable of."

Tolan shares seven ways to boost board member fundraising, both giving and getting:

1. **Clarity in recruitment.** If you expect board members to be active fundraisers, make that clear in the recruitment process, says Tolan. "You can't wait until the end of the year or start of a capital campaign to tell new members that you expect 100 percent board participation."

2. **Minimum giving.** Further clarify expectations with annual board commitment agreements of at least the nonprofit's minimum club level. Board members' presence in a legacy society will also strengthen requests for planned gifts.

3. **Campaign giving goals.** Goals and stretch goals for board giving in capital campaigns promote board giving, says Tolan. Be specific. "Setting numeric goals like raising $100,000 from your board's 20 members gives a very clear sense of individual obligations."

4. **Board expansion.** One simple way to increase board giving is to increase board size. Larger boards amplify fundraising potential while enhancing governance by allowing groups of members to specialize in areas such as publicity or fundraising.

5. **Thank-a-thon.** For boards with a weak culture of fundraising, Tolan says a thank-a-thon can be a great first step. Create a list of all donors from the past three months and have board members take turns making thank-you calls.

6. **Fundraising committee.** A dedicated fundraising committee can sharpen board members' attention on the issue, he says. Have the committee submit regular reports, put those reports at the beginning of the agenda and celebrate all levels of success.

7. **Cleaning house.** It's never too late to start building strong giving habits, but it might be too late for certain individuals, says Tolan. Replacing board members who have no history of annual giving and no desire to give to capital campaigns with more involved supporters can transform a board and, ultimately, a nonprofit.

### Board Giving by the Numbers

Every nonprofit wants actively giving board members, but details behind that goal can be fuzzy. These are some of the numeric benchmarks Justin Tolan, chief fundraising adviser at ME&V (Cedar Falls, IA), shares with clients:

- **100:** Percent of board members who should be giving to capital campaigns to maximize external fundraising.

- **10-15:** Percent of a campaign goal that should be collectively contributed by board members.

- **30:** Percent of a campaign goal that can often be raised by gifts from board members, staff and auxiliary volunteers.

- **15-20:** Minimum number of board members Tolan recommends for adequately shouldering fundraising and other responsibilities.

- **100:** Percent of staff that increasing numbers of donors want to see giving to a capital campaign.

*Source: Justin Tolan, Chief Fundraising Adviser, ME&V, Cedar Falls, IA. Phone (319) 268-9151. E-mail: jtolan@MEandV.com. Website: www.MEandV.com*

## Teach Board Members to Nurture Relationships

Board members can play a powerful role in making introductions and cultivating relationships on your organization's behalf.

To make them more aware of their potential and assume a more proactive role in making introductions to and cultivating major gift prospects, follow these steps:

1. Regularly share lists of nondonor prospects with board members. Ask them to select names of individuals, businesses and/or foundations they are willing to cultivate in various ways.

2. Share examples of board members or other volunteers who took the time to introduce your charity, particularly those introductions that eventually resulted in major gifts.

3. Make board members aware that you, or another staff person, are ready and willing to accompany board members on visits to would-be donors.

4. Encourage working in pairs if they find doing so more comfortable or productive.

5. Compliment board members who are performing and producing as expected. Do so in the presence of other board members.

## Make Board Contacts Regular and Meaningful

How often do you make contact with board members on an individual basis?

If building a can-do board is a priority for you, then making time to meet one-on-one with board members should be a priority as well.

Individual contacts with board members help strengthen their relationship with your organization in many ways, including:

1. Educating board members on matters you consider to be priorities.

2. Demonstrating your interest in and appreciation for them.

3. Enabling you to learn more about your board members' skills, interests and circles of influence that may be of value to your cause.

Individual contacts with board members should be regular, but at irregular intervals and appropriate, not contrived. Each meeting should have a clear objective in mind: to ask for a commitment of time, to clarify an issue or to seek the board member's advice, for instance.

By planning and monitoring your meetings with individual board members, you will not only create a more cohesive board, but also motivate its members to new levels of involvement and ownership of your cause.

**YEARLY BOARD MEMBER CONTACT REPORT**

Board Member _____
For Year Ending _____

| | DATE OF CONTACT | CONTACT TYPE | OBJECTIVE | FOLLOW-UP | COMMENTS |
|---|---|---|---|---|---|
| JAN. | | | | | |
| FEB. | | | | | |
| MAR. | | | | | |
| APR. | | | | | |
| MAY | | | | | |
| JUNE | | | | | |
| JULY | | | | | |
| AUG. | | | | | |
| SEPT. | | | | | |
| OCT. | | | | | |
| NOV. | | | | | |
| DEC. | | | | | |

Contact Type
V = Personal Visit    T = Telephone    C = Correspondence

## Groom a Board Member Recruiter

If your board could use some beefing up — based on capacity to give — why not assign that duty to one existing board member who can make a long-term difference?

Meet with your best recruiter choice and explain that, over the next three years, you intend to add new board members who have the capacity to make major gifts. Share with the recruiter the gift range you have in mind.

Ask the board member to help identify, research and cultivate relationships with persons who fit your criteria for board members. Meet monthly or quarterly with the board member to review names and map out plans to introduce your organization to would-be board members. Once you and the board member feel right about a particular prospect, feed that person's name to your board nominating committee for consideration.

## Strengthen Board Member Solicitation Skills

To understand why board member solicitation can make or break fundraising efforts, consider the assertion of Jim Lyons, senior partner at Pride Philanthropy (Alpharetta, GA), that board members are five to 10 times more likely to get appointments with potential donors than development staff.

"It's easy to turn down a professional fundraiser. Their job is to get turned down," says Lyons. "But when a volunteer who is giving their own money to an organization calls and says 'This is really important, and I'd like to tell you about it,' people will usually make time to listen."

> *"First, make sure you always ask for a specific amount.... Second, when you have made the ask, just be quiet.... Last, make sure there is a specific follow-up plan that leaves the ball in your court."*

Lyons answers questions about the all-important task of creating competent and confident board member solicitors:

***What is the biggest obstacle to effective board member fundraising?***

"It often goes back to how they were recruited. All too often we are so focused on recruiting toward yes that we end up downplaying critical fundraising expectations. It gets us board members, but it sets our organizations up for failure."

***How should fundraising expectations be communicated to potential or new board members?***

"They need to be told there are different ways to help. Some people are good at identifying prospects, some are good at telling an organization's story, and some don't want to set up appointments or take hard questions, but are willing to look someone in the eye and make the ask. No one has to do all three, but all board members should know that they are expected to be contributing in at least one area."

***How should development staff assist board member solicitation?***

"They should first of all help board members develop a prospect list of three to five contacts. (Any more will look like a job, and the board member won't do it.) They should prepare the meeting materials, should expect to do much of the follow-up, and can, according to the board member's preference, attend meetings to answer detail questions and supply statistics. But they should never set up the meeting. If a staff member calls to make an appointment on someone's behalf, it defeats the whole purpose."

***What should board members know about closing solicitations?***

"There are three keys. First, make sure you always ask for a specific amount. When you offer a range, people will always migrate to the bottom end. Second, when you have made the ask, just be quiet. It can be hard to sit through the silence, but if you start talking, you'll often be talking them out of the gift. Last, make sure there is a specific follow-up plan that leaves the ball in your court — something like 'I understand this is a big decision. Tell me when you would like us to follow up with you.'"

***What would need to be included in training to build board members' solicitation skills?***

"It's nice to have a meeting strictly devoted to solicitation training. You will want to do some role play and practice in the meeting — pair everyone up so they are not performing in front of each other, but have each member play both the solicitor and the donor. People will resist, but they always say it was helpful after the fact."

***How do you establish an ongoing culture of board member fundraising?***

"It starts at the top. It needs to be an ongoing CEO message and needs to be an important part of board member orientation and training. It's a process that takes time. You can't just send a memo and say you've established a culture of philanthropy. It requires long-term commitment."

*Source: Jim Lyons, Senior Partner, Pride Philanthropy, Alpharetta, GA. Phone (888) 417-0707. E-mail: Pride1jim@aol.com. Website: www.pridephilanthropy.com*

## Help Board Members Make Asks

When it comes to asking others for gifts, do your board members drag their feet?

Christina Thrun, development and marketing director, Big Brothers Big Sisters of Northwestern Wisconsin (Eau Claire, WI), shares a method her organization uses to get board members over their hesitation and engaged in seeking gifts: The Big Magic Breakfast, which has helped board members raise nearly $250,000 since 2004.

The event is based on the Raising More Money or Benevon Model of fundraising, which trains and coaches nonprofit organizations to implement a mission-based system for raising sustainable funding from individual donors.

For the breakfast, board members serve as table captains and fill a table of seven by inviting friends and colleagues. Staff provides them with tools and information on how to ask guests to participate, which makes it easier for them. No mass invitations are sent out for the event, which is designed to generate multiple-year gifts.

The breakfast runs 7:30 to 8:30 a.m. and includes a program that is about 35 minutes long with speakers such as the organization's CEO and board president, a volunteer/mentor and someone involved in the school system who can speak to the organization's impact on students.

At the end of the program, table captains pass out pledge cards and the board president asks people to make a gift.

Thrun says, "This event is a bit more of a high-pressure ask, but it's not a direct ask. By doing this event, our board members don't have to visit with people one on one and ask them to make a gift. Many of our board members really like this event and have chosen these events over the one-on-one approach."

She says the event has also been popular among donors and invited guests. "We've received a lot of great feedback from guests, who indicate how moving the event is. We've yet to have an event with completely dry eyes."

*Source: Christina Thrun, Development and Marketing Director, Big Brothers Big Sisters Northwestern Wisconsin, Eau Claire, WI. Phone (715) 835-0161. E-mail: Christina.Thrun@bbbs.org*

## Six No-solicitation Ways to Get Board Members Fundraising

Prospering nonprofits invariably have board members actively engaged in fundraising. Getting to that point, though, is a challenge for many organizations.

Jean Block, president of Jean Block Consulting Inc. (Albuquerque, NM), offers six proven methods for involving board members in the fundraising process — none of which require them to ask their friends for money.

1. **Take on a thank-you campaign.** Gather your board, pull a list of top supporters from the donor database and start making thank-you calls. "The members make the call, sincerely thank the donor and, if appropriate, offer a story about how the organization is making a difference," Block says. "No soliciting allowed, even if the donor wanted to give." She recommends outlining a script for members, but not in writing, so calls sound natural and organic. She adds that scheduling a thank-you campaign 10 days to two weeks before a traditional campaign can significantly increase donations.

2. **Personally comment on appeal letters.** Handwritten comments from board members greatly increase the interest and readability of form letters, says Block. Use wide margins and plenty of white space, and don't worry if board members' notes obscure printed text — it only adds to the appeal.

3. **Investigate their company's gift-matching program.** Surprisingly few board members know who makes giving decisions at their place of employment, says Block. Of those who do, even fewer have taken the time to introduce themselves to that person. Give them an assignment to find out the decision maker(s), introduce themselves and report back.

4. **Leverage their online social networking.** Many board members use Facebook or other social networking services, but few make a point of using those venues to mention the organizations they serve, says Block. Encourage them to post updates about major events and meetings, or just when something touches their heart. She says even occasional posts by 15 board members can have a tangible impact.

5. **Host an event at their home or office.** Block says hosting an event can be a good way to involve reluctant board members. Staff members can make the ask if it is a fundraising event, but she says board members should truly be hosts, including inviting acquaintances and organizing and paying for the event.

6. **Underwrite the costs of an appeal campaign.** Some board members will never ask someone for money, but Block says that doesn't mean they can't underwrite the expenses —printing, postage, etc. — of those who will.

*Source: Jean Block, President, Jean Block Consulting Inc., Albuquerque, NM. Phone (505) 899-1520. E-mail: jean@jblockinc.com. Website: www.jblockinc.com*

# Fundraising Strategies for Small Shops

## GETTING THE MOST OUT OF VOLUNTEERS

*Augmenting paid staff with volunteer labor can expand organizational services and stretch limited resources. In addition to providing routine administrative support, volunteers can solicit by phone and mail, help produce and staff fundraising events, and even lead special campaigns. Make the most of your volunteer help by giving them the training, guidance and oversight found in the following articles — the tools they need to flourish.*

## Volunteers Deserve Your High Expectations

The saying, "We become products of our environment," rings especially true in the volunteer field.

If your expectations of volunteers are moderate at best, moderate performance is the best you will ever receive. If paid staff exhibit mediocre commitment toward their jobs and achievement of goals, how can you expect volunteers to do any more?

Instead, create an atmosphere of high expectations for volunteers. Then watch them rise to the occasion.

To help your volunteers become all that they can be, incorporate these management principles into your work with them:

❑ **Show volunteers what is expected of them.** Have clearly defined objectives for individual volunteers as well as structured committees and boards. This includes job descriptions as well as quantifiable goals for the year or the duration of a project.

❑ **Enlist one or two leaders to help elevate others to a new level of performance.** Share your expectations with those who can help motivate others. Ask them to focus their efforts on this task.

❑ **Recognize and reward those who are living up to expectations.** Whenever a volunteer demonstrates behavior exceeding your highest expectations, recognize him/her both individually and publicly. Consider offering incentives for those who meet incremental benchmarks as they progress toward stated goals.

❑ **Include volunteers and board members in the planning process.** If you want these people to own a higher level of involvement, they should be involved in shaping and determining objectives.

Expect great things of your volunteers. Model expected behavior for them. Be there to help them succeed. And when you see them meeting and exceeding your expectations, recognize them directly and through all appropriate means at your disposal.

## Inspire Your Gift Solicitors

Whether your goal is to train development staff, volunteers, or both, the process of inspiring achievement plays a key role in getting solicitors to make calls, confidently present their case and close more gifts. Know that anyone who feels inspired will pursue tasks with far greater passion.

Here are seven results-oriented strategies to use to inspire your team:

1. **Be a model of passion for your cause.** If you lack the missionary zeal needed to enthusiastically represent your charity, you can't expect the same of others.

2. **Offer a clear vision of a dynamic future.** Create a lofty but achievable strategic plan — one that depicts what your organization will look like in the future and what fulfilling its mission will achieve — so your sales force buys into making that dream a reality.

3. **Translate your institution's vision into goals.** Make what it is they will need to do (to turn vision into reality) obvious in their minds. Establish an annual operational plan that ties to your strategic plan, complete with quan-tifiable objectives, action plans, strategies and timetables.

4. **Empower your solicitation force with the authority and latitude to solve challenges.** Expect the very best of them and nothing less. Allow them the freedom to test their own styles and creativity.

5. **Assess your team's strengths and weaknesses individually.** Learn what brings out the best in them. By knowing what makes each team member click, you can help to eliminate weaknesses and focus their talents.

6. **Provide them with selling points.** It's up to you to pinpoint your organization's greatest strengths and accomplishments. What are they? Let other solicitors hear you touting those points so they can use them as well.

7. **Demonstrate your belief in them by offering regular praise and incentives.** When a volunteer completes his/her calls on time and with proficiency, let it be known. When a development officer makes a new face-to-face contact, pat him/her on the back. Develop a menu of surprise incentives to reward positive behavior.

GETTING THE MOST OUT OF VOLUNTEERS

## Report Form Helps Solicitors Fulfill Expectations

When enlisting board members and volunteers in gift solicitation, be sure to provide them with an easy-to-understand form they can use to fulfill what's expected of them.

Although you will no doubt send marketing materials, pledge forms and perhaps additional information with them on prospect calls, note that a prospect profile and solicitation report such as the template shown here will provide key information about the prospect and help volunteer solicitors stay on track throughout the solicitation process.

---

### PROSPECT PROFILE AND SOLICITATION REPORT
#### — FOR INDIVIDUALS —

Lead Solicitor _____

Secondary Solicitors_____

Prospect _____

Home Address_____

City _____ State _____ ZIP _____

Home Phone _____ E-mail_____

Business _____ Title_____

Business Address _____

Business Phone _____ E-mail_____

Spouse _____

Relationship to [Name of Charity] _____

#### 5-YEAR HISTORY OF CONTRIBUTIONS TO [NAME OF CHARITY]

| Year | Amount | Purpose |
|------|--------|---------|
| 2008 | $5,000 | Unrestricted (Annual Fund) |
| 2009 | $7,000 | Unrestricted (Annual Fund) |
| 2010 | $7,000 | Unrestricted (Annual Fund) |
| 2011 | $7,500 | Unrestricted (Annual Fund) |

Amount to be Solicited     $ _____

#### SOLICITATION RESULTS

Date of Solicitation _____

❏ Yes       Amount  $_____     Form of Gift _____
   If pledged, over what period of time? _____
   Beginning _____ Ending _____
   Use of gift _____
❏ No    Reason: _____
❏ Decision Pending    Planned Follow-up: _____
_____

Additional Comments Regarding Prospect: _____
_____
_____

*Please use back of form to record key discussion points of call. Return to [Name of Organization]*

---

## Give Volunteers Choices

Many hands make light work. Right?

Well, your work load may not get any lighter but, if you work smart, volunteers can certainly help in fund development.

Whether you're just beginning to enlist volunteers or building on an existing program, the number of participating volunteers will grow if you offer them a menu of ways in which to get involved.

Develop a checklist of fund development actions and share it with board members, existing donors and those who have been active volunteers with your cause. Agree to one or more ways in which these individuals could assist in your advancement efforts.

Here's a sampling of actions volunteers can select from:

❏ Sign appeal letters.
❏ Write personal notes of thanks.
❏ Make appointments for introductory calls.
❏ Establish a challenge gift.
❏ Make an annual and/or planned gift.
❏ Help cultivate major gift prospects.
❏ Review a proposal.
❏ Identify planned gift prospects.
❏ Act as hosts at fundraising events.
❏ Help rate/screen major gift prospects.
❏ Review/approve gift policies.
❏ Help with strategic planning.
❏ Serve on a search committee.
❏ Assist with tours.
❏ Chair your annual fund committee.

Any involvement in the fundraising process will help make these persons more gift-conscious and more willing to take on additional fundraising assignments.

## Six Tips for Training First-time Solicitors

As head of a small army of volunteer class agents soliciting on behalf of Dickinson College (Carlisle, PA), Stacy Paul, associate director of annual giving, knows a bit about training novice solicitors.

Here, she shares six tips that have placed her in good stead with this important aspect of organizational fundraising:

1. **Convey expectations.** Explaining expectations up front is important for retaining volunteers, says Paul. She has used an online handbook, tips and talking points, and a Microsoft PowerPoint presentation for training, but stresses that one-on-one meetings cannot be replaced.

2. **Focus training on priority concerns.** The biggest lesson Paul tries to impress on rookies is the importance of every gift. The more they understand this, she says, the more they can help potential donors appreciate the importance of even a $25 or $10 gift. She also makes a point to overcome volunteer reluctance to make a specific dollar-figure ask.

3. **Carefully structure volunteer time and tasks.** Dickinson volunteers spend one week each month on donor stewardship (appreciation calls, thank-you notes, etc.) and one on direct solicitation. "Keeping volunteers busy not only benefits the college, it makes them feel needed and valuable," she says.

4. **Communicate pertinent information.** Though class agents work largely independently, Paul, keeps in touch through personal calls and e-mail, as well as through newsletters at the end of the calendar and fiscal years, quarterly and midyear updates. Providing information on funding, goals and campus events, these updates keep volunteers motivated and supplied with information that can be used in solicitation conversations.

5. **Vary training by giving levels.** Though most class agents focus on relatively small gifts, some volunteers target upper-level donors as well. These receive more in-depth training from an assigned leadership giving officer and sometimes travel with that officer to observe and take part in in-person solicitations.

6. **Adapt to the times.** Though most solicitation is still done by phone, volunteers are increasingly contacting donors through e-mail and even Facebook. Because this has created a somewhat more relaxed solicitation environment, Paul says development professionals should keep abreast of such changing norms.

*Source: Stacy Paul, Associate Director of Annual Giving, Dickinson College, Carlisle, PA. Phone (800) 543-3809. E-mail: Pauls@dickinson.edu*

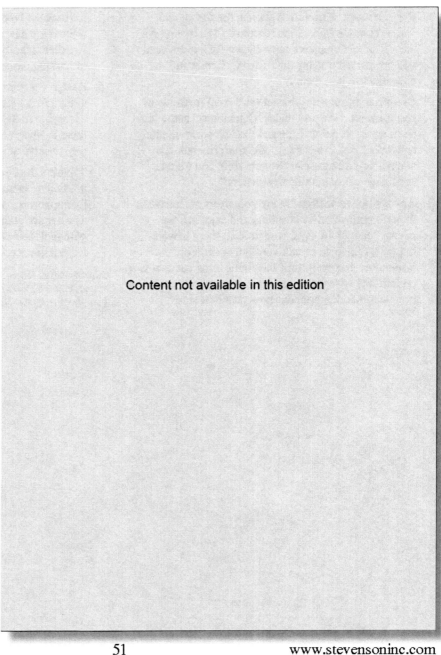

Content not available in this edition

## Seven Tips to Recruit and Retain Special Event Volunteers

Produced by the La Quinta Arts Foundation (La Quinta, CA), the 29-year-old La Quinta Arts Festival is widely considered by both artists and art patrons alike to be one of the best annual festivals of its kind nationwide. The four-day event attracts about 20,000 visitors per year and has been named a Top 10 festival by numerous arts publications.

The arts festival is also one of the La Quinta Arts Foundation's biggest fundraisers.

Christi Salomone, the arts foundation's executive director, estimates about 300 volunteers work on the festival each year. Here, she shares seven ideas for recruiting and retaining a large number of dedicated volunteers for your large special events:

1. **Rely on word of mouth.** Although the foundation does recruit through various methods, Salomone says most festival volunteers come by way of experienced volunteers encouraging their friends, family and colleagues to join them.

2. **Use other community-based (and free) methods of recruitment.** "We post under 'Community' in the local newspaper, on our website and through social-media networks," Salomone says. "We give presentations at other service agencies (Rotary, etc.), and we take advantage of community newsletters."

3. **Always be recruiting.** "Many volunteers are introduced to our organization by attending and enjoying our events," Salomone says, "which leads them to want to play a role in an event's continuing success." Remember that every time the public turns out, that is an opportunity to recruit — and that every public event you produce should, therefore, show your best side.

4. **Look across the age spectrum.** "We are lucky to live in an area desirable to active retirees," says Salomone, which leads to a high turnout of older volunteers. Try focusing your volunteer-recruitment efforts at retirement centers, churches and the like. Another tactic: For volunteer duties that could be carried out by a family acting as a unit, pitch yourself to PTA groups, schools, or, again, churches. If you have teen-friendly volunteer duties, see if your local high school or church youth group can help you out, as some require young people to fulfill volunteer-service duties.

5. **Prepare them!** You'd be surprised how many nonprofits recruit volunteers for an event and then just tell them to show up. Not at La Quinta — volunteers are given written job descriptions and orientation meetings. Another amenity volunteers enjoy: assigned parking and/ or parking passes.

6. **Assign everyone a leader.** A critical reason that the La Quinta Arts Festival's volunteers return year after year, according to Salomone is, "Our volunteers know that there is always a go-to staff person on whom they can rely to solve any issue."

7. **Thank volunteers the same as you do donors.** After all, time is money. "We acknowledge their contributions by imparting a personal touch," says Salomone, "such as a handwritten thank-you note. We find volunteers who feel their contributions are valued and have a good experience are likely to return year after year."

*Source: Christi Salomone, Executive Director, La Quinta Arts Foundation, La Quinta, CA. Phone (760) 564-1244. E-mail: Christi@lqaf.com. Website: www.lqaf.com*

# Fundraising Strategies for Small Shops

## LEVERAGING THE POWER OF SOCIAL MEDIA

*A few short years ago social media platforms such as Facebook and Twitter were a mere novelty. No more. Social media has transformed age-old patterns of communication, and only to the extent that nonprofits master these emerging tools will they be able to sustain long-term success. Whether for fundraising, friendraising, outreach or recruiting, social media is a force no organization can afford to ignore or fail to exploit.*

## Three Reasons to Spend Time on Regular Online Networking

So you're sitting at your desk with a few minutes to spare. You open up your Facebook page. Guilty pleasure or smart business move?

Smart move, definitely, says Mandy Wittschen, feature article writer, Haley Marketing Group (Avon, OH): "I liken it to regular exercise. The more effort you put into your online networking, the greater the results you'll see."

Wittschen says the following three options are just a small portion of the opportunities that await you online.

1. **Positioning yourself as an expert** by writing and posting articles, sharing links to helpful content or answering a question.
2. **Drawing traffic to your website or professional blog.**
3. **Taking advantage of viral marketing.** Facebook allows you to develop applications that sit on other people's profile pages where they can invite others to include the application on their own pages — all with no work from you.

While the possibilities for using online networks to promote your organization and its efforts are endless, your time is not. Wittschen recommends thoroughly researching networks, then focusing your efforts on one or two that best match your needs.

*Source: Mandy Wittschen, Feature Article Writer, Haley Marketing Group, Avon, OH. Phone (888) 696-2900.*
*E-mail: mwittschen000@centurytel.net*

## Poll Audiences, Then Choose Social Media

Thinking of creating an organizational presence on a social networking site? Streamline your efforts by first polling your audiences to see which site they prefer, then focus on that one first.

In April 2009, staff with College of the Mainland (Texas City, TX) posted a week-long poll on their home page asking users to choose the online social networking site they used most: Facebook, Flickr, MySpace, Twitter, YouTube or none.

"We wanted to see where we could do some potential advertising and where to reach our students and potential students on the Web," says Lana Pigao, director of marketing and publications. She notes that at the time, the only site the college used was Facebook.

Poll responses were recorded in a database and analyzed when the college created its annual marketing plan and budget.

Pigao says the college chose to create an online poll instead of a traditional poll to add an interactive and fun element to their website.

The marketing and communications staff created poll questions, and the college webmaster used Poll Daddy (www.polldaddy.com), which offers free and paid accounts that allow users to create polls and surveys, to create the poll.

*Source: Lana Pigao, Director of Marketing and Publications, College of the Mainland, Texas City, TX.*
*Phone (409) 938-1211, ext. 434. E-mail: lpigao@com.edu*

## Build Workable Social Media Strategy

While social media is new territory for many membership organizations, its underlying strategy is not as foreign as some might imagine, says David Sieg, vice president of strategic marketing, YourMembership.com, Inc. (St. Petersburg, FL).

"Start a social media strategy by defining a concrete goal — a membership level, dollar figure, etc. — that is quantifiable and has a relatively short-term end date, maybe a year to 18 months," Sieg says.

The next step, he says, is devising objectives, both social and traditional, that further this goal. "If your goal is achieving X number of members by 2012, you might say you will send Y direct mail pieces, launch a social media marketing campaign via Twitter and LinkedIn, and commit Z dollars to advertising."

Finally, devise operational tactics supporting each objective. This planning process must include development of a defined content strategy.

"Firing random thoughts out across Twitter will not get the job done," says Sieg. "You need a consistent voice, a consistent message and a consistency of communication across many kinds of media. An annual schedule of communication, detailing by quarter or month what will be sent out to whom by what portal, is an invaluable part of any social media initiative."

*Source: David Sieg, Vice President, Strategic Marketing, YourMembership.com, Inc., St. Petersburg, FL. Phone (727) 827-0046.*
*E-mail: dsieg@yourmembership.com*

## Social Media Strategies That Increase Visibility

Far from being a passing fad, social media is rapidly extending into the corporate and nonprofit sectors and changing the way stakeholders communicate with each other, and how they expect to communicate with your organization.

What is social media? It is using the Internet to instantly collaborate, share information and have a conversation about ideas, causes and organizations we care about powered by social media tools (e.g., social networking sites, blogs, podcasts, etc.).

Holly Ross, executive director, NTEN: The Nonprofit Technology Network (Portland, OR), says nonprofit communicators must understand how social media's newfound popularity will impact their cause and relay that to their constituency.

"As nonprofits, we're used to being authorities to our communities," Ross says. "Our role has been to decide what's important regarding our issues, to tell our community what matters and to organize them to create change."

But the development of the Internet has forced nonprofits to change how they relate to their communities, she says: "First, the Internet has made accessing information incredibly easy. If you want to know about logging in your state, Google will tell you what's going on. Second (and this is the newest part), the Internet has made it ridiculously easy for us to share that information with each other, and to organize around that information.

"What that means is that people don't need us to tell them what matters. They don't need us to organize them. So as nonprofits our value proposition has shifted. We need to learn how they are using these tools to organize themselves, and what they are saying about our issues, so we can understand what value we can bring to them."

Ross emphasizes that nonprofit communicators should think of social media as a series of steps that must be taken to increase visibility:

1. **Listen and participate in conversations that are already happening.** First, find out and listen to what people are talking about regarding the issues about which you care. How are they talking about the issues? What's motivating them? Next, use that knowledge to share your own insights and resources.

2. **Share your story.** Once you have a feel for the conversation, get your own story out there via blogs, podcasts, videos, etc. and invite the community to participate. Be brave and create content that is appropriate for your audiences and encourages feedback and conversation.

3. **Generate buzz.** Use sites like Facebook, StumbleUpon, Digg and Twitter to tell the world about what you're doing. Build a community of peers on these sites that will help you get the word out about your stories to their networks.

"The key to all these is community," says Ross. "You have to build real relationships with real people to make it work. That means that you'll have to contribute as much as you take, and you'll have to be open to whatever the community wants to tell you."

*Source: Holly Ross, Executive Director, NTEN: The Nonprofit Technology Network, Portland, OR. Phone (415) 397-9000. E-mail: holly@nten.org*

### Social Media's Challenges

Like many forms of communication, social media has its pros and cons, says Holly Ross, executive director, NTEN: The Nonprofit Technology Network (Portland, OR).

Ross offers an example of how social media has changed communications for the better in terms of speed and scope: "We always wanted to create that perfect viral e-mail that would get forwarded around the Web. Adding 25 people to an e-mail send list is tedious compared to adding a link to Digg (www.digg.com). Getting your networks to tell a friend is all about capitalizing on their emotions in the moment. The easier that is, the more you'll get out of it. And social media makes it very easy."

While social media has helped in this manner, she notes it isn't a panacea. Its pitfalls include:

✓ **Presenting challenges to an organization's many cultures.** "To successfully implement a social media strategy, your organization must be prepared to behave in new ways. You have to be much more open and transparent than many organizations have been up to this point. The idea of accepting comments on a blog is abhorrent to many organizations, for example. They can't bear the idea of someone saying something negative."

✓ **Lack of control.** "The biggest mistake I see organizations make is the attempt to control their social media strategy too much. That's not how social media works. You can't delete negative comments. You have to respond to them honestly and openly."

✓ **Social media structure vs. organizational structure.** "We're used to working in departmental silos; program does program work, fundraising raises money, marketing tells our stories. Social media combine elements of all of those.... The folks implementing social media strategies are crossing departments more frequently, challenging our old ways of getting work done."

## Look to Social Media to Expand Your Fundraising Reach

Social media is one of the trendiest ways nonprofits can raise funds. But with your budget and staff already stretched, how can you implement social media into your efforts?

Take a cue from Big Brothers Big Sisters of America (BBBS), a Philadelphia, PA-based nonprofit that uses many social media venues. Here, Cheyenne Palma, director of development, shares what works for the organization:

**Twitter is one of the largest online social networking sites, and it's easy to get lost in all the tweets. How do you use this site productively?**

"We try to tweet once a day during the work week and we only follow legitimate people who follow us (trying to avoid the spammers) and we also follow up with a direct message to further engage new followers."

**Facebook is another site that is seeing exponential growth. How does your Facebook fan page work for you?**

"We have 4,035 fans, an increase of more than 40 percent for the year and our Facebook Causes site (a part of Facebook that allows 501(c)(3) organizations to receive donations through Facebook) currently has 1,896 members who have donated $613. To keep the fan page current and reduce time spent on it, we simply integrated our RSS feed into the site. We've also learned much of our current donor base is active on Facebook and through research and data analysis, we have located nearly 20 percent of them on the site. We've recently formalized our efforts to invite them to connect with us on Facebook."

**LinkedIn is known more for its corporate network and as a place for like-minded business people to connect. Do you feel nonprofit fundraising has a place on LinkedIn?**

"We are still in the very early stages of determining how we will use LinkedIn. We've begun to identify board members and donors who are active on LinkedIn, but have yet to complete this analysis. We have discussed using the Events module and the Groups functionality to connect with specific donors and supporters on LinkedIn. We anticipate this will be a much more targeted effort and not as broad an approach as Facebook."

**It seems that cell phones can do just about everything now, including depositing paychecks online. Will BBBS dip its toes in the mobile giving waters?**

"We are now piloting the ability to donate funds via texting and we have 11 agencies testing text giving. Primarily, we are testing its usage at local events, such as radiothons and baseball games. It appears there is potential where we have a very large, captive audience. Our East Tennessee affiliate received 83 donations in response to a recent radiothon in their market.

"We also anticipate folding mobile giving into our social media fundraising efforts through fundraising widgets. By placing a text-giving widget on select sites, viewers won't even need to go to a separate donation page to contribute; they can simply send a text."

**What do you think is important for nonprofits venturing into social media to remember? And if they're not already doing it, should they be?**

"It's very important for nonprofits to be involved in social media, particularly because it's the wave of the future. If you look at future generations of donors, it's how they communicate.

"An exaggerated example of this was demonstrated in a news article I read online recently about two teenage girls in Australia trapped in a storm drain — they updated their Facebook status instead of dialing for help! This is the future donor base that fundraisers are looking at tapping into; they need to get on board now, even if it's just to get their name and their message out there.

"Even from a budgetary perspective it makes sense: a few personnel hours per week can lead to donations that you might not otherwise have gotten, and there's no outside overhead to set it up or maintain it if you do it all in-house."

*Source: Cheyenne Palma, Director of Development, Big Brothers Big Sisters, Philadelphia, PA. Phone (215) 665-7765, E-mail: cheyenne.palma@bbbs.org*

## Analyze Social Media Efforts to Measure Return On Investment

You begin by placing an important announcement on your organization's website. Next, you tweet a link to the announcement asking your Twitter followers to check it out. A few days later, you post a synopsis of the announcement on your blog, including a link to the original Web page. You might even send another tweet announcing the blog post.

And because you integrated Twitter into your LinkedIn and Facebook pages, additional fans, friends and contacts receive the news through those outlets.

Such cross-fertilization makes for good communication strategy while providing a body of concrete metrics to gauge social media efforts' effectiveness, says David Sieg, vice president of strategic marketing, YourMembership.com, Inc. (St. Petersburg, FL).

Sieg says the following areas are particularly suited to measurement:

✓ **Inbound clicks.** The amount of traffic social media communications are driving to your website is an important measure of overall impact, says Sieg. How many users are clicking through to your site from your blog? From your Twitter tweets? From your Facebook page? Measure this information and use it.

✓ **Industry links.** Links are the mark of online relevance, and the number of industry groups and prominent bloggers who link to your website suggests the regard in which your organization (or at least its published content) is held, says Sieg.

✓ **Audience.** Whether friends or fans, subscribers or followers, your loyal audience members are another easily tabulated metric. But Sieg cautions that readership is only a first step, and that user-initiated interaction — filling out a contact page, downloading a contact form, reposting your article — should be the primary goal.

✓ **Search engine optimization.** Your organization's organic page rank (the place it appears on a search engine's page of unpaid search results) is a matter of great importance, says Sieg. Not only does it reflect the number of people viewing your content and linking to your posts, it determines how easily potential members will be able to find your online presence. Never ignore a rising or falling page rank.

✓ **Website analytics.** Google Analytics (www.google.com/analytics), the gold standard of free website analysis, can determine many metrics including clicks, links and referring sites. Website usage patterns revealed by online analytics (how long users view a page, what pages users leave your website from, what percentage of users landing on a contact page fill out the form) also give clues into user preferences and behavior.

Finally, Sieg says, do not ignore conventional metrics. "Is your membership growing? Is your revenue increasing? Are your services being utilized?" These are areas on which social media should be having an impact and warrant another form of measurement.

*Source: David Sieg, Vice President, Strategic Marketing, YourMembership.com, Inc., St. Petersburg, FL. Phone (727) 827-0046. E-mail: dsieg@yourmembership.com. Website: www.yourmembership.com*

Lightning Source UK Ltd.
Milton Keynes UK
UKOW01f0823020813

214783UK00006B/169/P